Finders & Keepers

How the World's Most Powerful Customer
is Changing Everything

By Rob Schlyecher

Library and Archives Canada Cataloguing in Publication

Schlyecher, Rob, 1962-, author

Finders & Keepers : how the world's most powerful customer is changing everything / Rob Schlyecher.

Includes bibliographical references.

ISBN 978-0-9940593-0-7 (pbk.)

1. Marketing. 2. Branding (Marketing). I. Title.

HF5415.S34 2015   658.8   C2015-901144-2

Editing by Carole Audet
Book design by Jeremy Grice
Cover photo by Raeff Miles

If you would like to publish sections of this book,
please contact the publisher for permission.

Published by:
Spring Advertising Ltd.
Rob Schlyecher
301-1250 Homer St.
Vancouver, BC, V6B 1C6
Phone: 604-863-0167 x 303
rob@springadvertising.com

To my Wife. Thanks for finding me.

Contents

FOREWORD

In a world filled with data and opinions, what entrepreneurs, business owners and marketing professionals really need is insight, and the ability to execute on it. This meeting of science and art is precisely what Rob Schlyecher lays out in this book. We all know that some companies are able to achieve significantly higher revenues and margins for products that customers rave about, even when up against bigger more powerful brands. Unlocking the people who drive these business successes - the customers, and how you actually go about appealing to them, is the real art that Rob is the master of.

Too often great ideas go through the marketing and product development sausage machine and end up looking like everything else. Thankfully now, through the pathway Rob lays out, for those with the balls to do what is right as opposed to what they have done in the past, that doesn't have to happen anymore.

Christopher Norton, CEO Crowdspending Inc. & Author, One Hundred Thirteen Million Markets of One.

INTRODUCTION

What's not to love about a generalization? In demographics it can be a comfortable blanket statement that helps us to gain a broad understanding of the behaviors and values of each generation. There is the Baby Boomer, there is Generation X and Generation Y. Now there is a new one, the Millennial. And "new" can be a problem. This is because, time being what it is, each new "generational generalization" comes with a lack of historical data. Misconceptions can only follow. So at the core of any examination of the Millennial sits this misconception: the behavior of Millennials can be understood and predicted through demographics. It can't.

Instead they can be clearly understood by learning from another kind of person – one who transcends descriptions based on age, income, education or gender. In this way the blueprint for the Millennial consumer has been written by a consumer who drives the success of almost every thriving business that exists today. This is the confident, individualistic spender whose purchasing power drove trend-busting growth for a select group of businesses right through the worst recession in seventy years. You are about to meet the Finder.

But first, a little (recent) history.

A lot can happen in a decade. Back in 2005, you could jump in your new Pontiac and take a drive over to the supercenter for a look at DVD players at Circuit City. After that, you could stroll over to Linens N Things for a new set of bed sheets. Then, push your cart out the door and roll past that giant new Bombay Company megastore. At some point you might have waved at your brother-in-law as he cruised the parking lot for a spot big enough to hold his newly leased Hummer. Back then he was earning a good living at Bonanza Steak House.

A lot can happen in *under* a decade. Pontiac, Circuit City, Linens N Things, Bombay Company, Hummer, and Bonanza Steak House were gone by 2013. What erased these brands and their deceased contemporaries from the early 21st century landscape? Could their collective demise be explained by changes in technology, or excessive competition, shifting demographics, tightening of credit, the real estate crash, or that catch-all answer, the recession? The answer is none of the above.

Ten years ago there was an Apple, but there were few Apple Stores. Chipotle Mexican Grill was still a slightly obscure little chain of burrito joints. Subaru held a tenuous foothold on North American soil and an Audi was the exclusive driving domain of the turtlenecked architect. A smattering of Anthropologie stores were just beginning to sell their scarves, dresses, and candles. Whole Foods and its like were moving out of granola-covered hippy-dom into the mainstream. Craft beer was no more than the beverage of choice for bearded men of the socks-in-sandals variety.

Everything has changed. Today, Apple Stores are the one and only uncontested and unchallenged sales-per-square-foot juggernaut. Subaru and Audi have built on their almost freakish avoidance of the last recession. Chipotle is enjoying double-digit sales growth on $9 burritos throughout their 1,500 plus network. This is while cut-priced fast feeders watch their sales numbers fall into the deep fryer. An Anthropologie store is thriving in a mall near you.

Success and failure: all part of the natural cycle of business. But today, it isn't necessarily true. There is a key to the success of almost every business that profits, grows, thrives, employs, and flourishes today. To hold that key is to have the power to avoid the pitfalls of the last ten years and the years to come. It is the key to profitable and lasting business success.

The key is a customer. A type of customer who drives the unprecedented growth of craft brewing while branded beer sales go flat. This is the customer who bought a Subaru at full price back in 2008 while deeply discounted Chryslers gathered dust on bankrupted car lots. Today this is the only customer who matters – the customer who does more than 75% of the discretionary spending in America. Get ready. The two of you are about to meet. What you will learn will change everything.

It only took 840,000,000 data points

In 2002, Australian social scientist, Ross Honeywill, and research company, Roy Morgan International, began a study that would track behavioral and attitudinal data on 100,000 adults on an annual basis in North America, Europe, Australia, and Asia over a ten-year period. The study used eighty-four attitudinal factors and one hundred behavioral factors to examine consumer habits, lifestyle, attitudes toward careers, information, self-determination, and a wide range of related characteristics.

By 2006, Honeywill had gathered five years worth of data, adding up to 500,000 respondents. Once analyzed through those one hundred behavioral factors and eighty-four attitudinal factors, a set of data was produced and the first part of the study was completed. It revealed something extraordinary one of the most powerful consumers that the world has ever seen. A consumer who spends more readily, does not make purchase decisions based on price or status and even views the concept of time in a slightly different way. What Honeywill had discovered was a consumer who represents just 24 percent of the North American adult population but is responsible for a hugely outsized bulk of discretionary spending. This segment isn't necessarily wealthy, but is generally financially successful and even that success comes from a whole set of factors identified in the study. Honeywill called this segment of the population, the New Economic Order, or NEO for short.

On the other side of his findings lived an entirely different kind of consumer. This consumer was found to hold a more traditional outlook on life and to consume more reluctantly, only moved by a set of stimulants that include a low price, a brand that helps to lend the buyer identity, a "bang-for-the-buck" stack of features in any purchase, and even the status of ownership. Honeywill's study reported that this consumer represents 52 percent of the North American adult population but only 23 percent of discretionary spending. He called this consumer the "Traditional."

Finally, Honeywill's study unearthed a third kind of consumer – one that exhibits the same attitudes and values as the NEO but lacks the spending power to consume at the same rate. Members of this group, now named the Evolving NEOs or Evolvers, were found to represent the remaining 22 percent of the adult population and, while lacking the spending power of the NEO, still spend at a rate that eclipses that of the Traditional. Between them, and their 46 percent portion of the adult population, NEOs and Evolvers represent 77 percent of all discretionary spending in North America.

In 2006, Honeywill and partner, Verity Byth, published their findings on this powerful consumer segment in their home country of Australia with an appropriate proportion of home turf content. The book is titled, *NEO Power: How the New Economic Order Is Changing the Way We Live, Work, and Play.*

In 2008, British expat, Christopher Norton, now a California resident, discovered the NEO research work and developed a working relationship with Honeywill. Together the two picked up the still running NEO study and brought it to North America. By 2012, they had gathered a total of one million respondents over a ten-year period and run them through the same data points that had been introduced a decade earlier. The results were shocking in their consistency. NEOs and Evolvers still spend at a rate that makes up 77 percent of discretionary spending in America. Traditionals in America spend at a rate that represents just 23 percent.

With those one million respondents, eighty-four attitudinal factors, and one hundred behavioral characteristics, the pair had accumulated a data set of 840 million data points spread across four continents. These results were then evaluated by global audit and accounting firm KPMG. The firm compared them to standard U.S. research models like Yankelovich. KPMG then declared the results of the NEO study to be among the most usable and robust models available.

Then Christopher Norton, armed with the study's findings, did something that took the study out of academia and into an actual market. He put the data to work. By using NEO data, Norton, while serving as lead marketing strategist to Four Seasons Private Residences Denver, was able to build and execute a marketing strategy and plan that yielded results that were nothing short of miraculous. In less than eighteen months, Norton's NEO-based action plan would sell out a just-recently-failing real estate development filled with million dollar plus condominiums, without employing any significant discounts, and during the worst property recession the country had seen in almost eighty years. This was accomplished while no other luxury properties in the Greater Denver area sold at all!

Norton was now the man who could not only talk the NEO talk, he could walk the NEO walk. His own book, co-authored with Honeywill and published in 2012, titled *One Hundred Thirteen Million Markets of One: How the New Economic Order Can Remake the American Economy*, takes the now extensive study's results and, among its many insights, puts them in an American context. The book describes real-life NEO situations, observations on companies that get it right the NEO way, and the many who get it wrong. Norton also lays out the powerful and sustainably positive financial implications of a properly recognized and supported NEO economy.

In 2008, Vancouver based strategy and advertising firm, Spring Advertising Ltd., began its work with Norton using the NEO findings. Spring Partner, Richard Bergin, with his MBA thesis in alternative market research techniques, began to translate the study's data into a highly effective advertising and marketing tool. Since then Richard, James Filbry, and I have worked extensively with Christopher Norton using the NEO data.

The partners at Spring Advertising Ltd. share a combined sixty-five years and counting in advertising and brand strategy. We three have worked on brands and products that stretch from the global to the Mom and Pop. Their creative work has been recognized internationally and awarded for excellence by such respected bodies as Communication Arts, London International Awards, and The One Show.

This book is the culmination of the NEO research, deep marketing experience across years, industries, countries, and markets, and a growing impatience with the failings of traditional advertising.

Enjoy.

Vancouver, August 14, 2015

1

◆

THE $4.7 TRILLION CARTON OF EGGS

Where We Meet the Finder – the Most Valuable Customer on the Planet

You can tell a lot about a person by watching them buy eggs.

It is a Sunday afternoon and you are standing on the glossy linoleum of pretty much any supermarket in pretty much any neighborhood in America. The automatic doors swish back and forth as shoppers walk in and out. They are here to get ready for tonight's dinner and stock up for the week ahead. Take a stroll over to the dairy section. You will see eggs stacked neatly in the upright coolers. Some are popular brands packaged in sterile looking Styrofoam flats, others in dozen packs of rough, recycled-looking cardboard. A woman, let's call her Tina, rolls up with her cart and scans the wide variety. Watch carefully and you will see that her gaze rarely touches the white eggs in their white Styrofoam flats. She seems more interested in those rough cardboard containers. She picks one up, opens it, and glances at the deep tan colored, slightly speckled, and faintly misshapen eggs inside. The nicely designed type on the package speaks of free-range chickens and organic origins. Satisfied, Tina places these in her cart without so much as a glance at the price. Price wasn't part of her little shopping moment. Price was not what convinced her to buy these eggs.

While we were there, so was Lloyd. His cart was parked right next to Tina's. Like Tina, he bought eggs. Unlike Tina, his eggs were purchased for a whole different set of reasons. We will return to Lloyd and his eggs a little later. Tina gets to go first. Here's why.

Tina is what we will now call a Finder. As a Finder, Tina could very well represent the most important consumer alive today. She and her fellow Finders are the economic force that is shaping our economy. Finders have created dramatic and even gaudy business success stories across America and all over the world over the past two decades and many of those success stories have taken place in the face of the greatest economic recession to occur since the world stopped calling them depressions.

Tina belongs to a group of 113 million Americans who live, think, and buy differently. They can be defined by the way that they use, enjoy, and spend their discretionary income. Fifty-nine million of them are Finders and a further fifty-four million are what we will be calling Evolving Finders. Finders and Evolving Finders make up 46 percent of the adult population of the United States. Their discretionary spending power is simply gigantic at 4.7 trillion dollars a year. In spite of the fact that Finders and Evolving Finders represent just under half of the population, they account for 77 percent of all discretionary spending in this country today.

Let us allow those numbers to sink in for a moment – 77 percent of discretionary spending – $4.7 trillion – 113 million adults. Those are big figures. Of course they beg the most obvious question: How could so many people, who spend so much money, so often, ever be overlooked? There are a number of reasons.

Until now, Finders have not been considered a market because our conventional ways of measuring consumers and their behaviors have failed to identify their common characteristics as any sort of pattern. This is understandable. For all their size and power, Finders cannot be treated as a target market. Each one is an individual and by that very definition is highly individualistic. Yet they can be found, and they are communicated with and are sold to like no other.

There are companies that understand Finders innately. In fact Finders might be individualistic but all of the companies that have any sense of their existence, and act accordingly, understand that they share a common and much less individualistic characteristic: profitability.

When organizations define themselves along strong philosophical and value lines that appeal to Finders, they are indeed highly profitable and have proven themselves to be almost entirely recession-proof. That may in fact be an understatement. These companies, big and small, regional and global, have continued to thrive while other businesses around them have flat-lined and disappeared from the streets, shopping centers, and auto malls of our world. You will know some of these strong few: Apple, Anthropologie, Audi, Subaru, Lululemon. There are also the small successes that thrive in your own neighborhood and those that you may not be aware of like a little chocolate store behind an auto mall, or an Italian grocer on a busy street. There is much to be learned from all of them. And, there is much to be gleaned from those who failed. That is not to say that Finders are the harbinger of riches for one and all; there are businesses that thrive by doing what Finders would avoid at all costs. But let's get back to Tina.

Tina is one among 113 million people. Her upper income puts her among the first and most powerful category of Finders – those who flex spending power far beyond their 20 percent share of the U.S. population. The balance of that 113 million is represented by Evolving Finders, a group that is largely comprised of members of the millenial demographic and exhibits Finder attitudes and habits but lacks the buying power at this point in their lives to behave exactly like Finders. Together they're an engine that drives the fortunes of a broad spectrum of organizations and companies. They can also deliver failure to companies who neglect their characteristics and values.

Found

1) There are 113 million adults in America alone who look on spending with values that transcend price and features.

2) Fifty-nine million of these people are high income earning,

high spending Finders who, with their fifty-four million less-moneyed, more millenial cousins:

a) represent 46 percent of the adult population

b) account for a disproportionate 77 percent of discretionary spending, and

c) $4.7 trillion dollars in annual spending.

3) Finders are strongly individualistic but have a value set that aligns with certain companies big and small that in turn creates incredibly successful and recession-proof businesses.

2

◆

DEMOGRAPHICS SCHMEMOGRAPHICS

Family Un-Resemblance

Claire is Tina's little sister. She's younger by just two years, which puts Claire at 39 and Tina at 41. As it stands, Claire holds the bragging rights to the fact that unlike her sister Tina, she's still in her thirties. Of course, this is a difference that isn't much of a difference at all – not even to a demographer. But there are other differences that have nothing to do with age or any other measurable qualities. Unfortunately, those are easily and often overlooked. Claire and Tina have a similar level of education. Both had pretty average childhoods with the usual balance of function and dysfunction in their family. The two even hold a strong family resemblance. Both are married. Both have children. A demographer might classify them as carbon copies. And, that demographer would be right within his or her definition. Age, gender, education, income, and family are the five common demographic measurements that have acted as the standard measurements inside of the marketer's world for decades. They have been the crystal ball through which countless businesses have examined the present, tried to learn from the past, and attempted to predict the future. The trouble is what they measure is usually irrelevant. This is because demographics can do very little to transcend objective limitations beyond their own dimensions. They can tell how old you are but they can't tell how old you feel. They can organize you by education level but they can't tell if you showed up for all your classes. Demographics will predict that these two sisters will behave in exactly the same way. Common sense and plain old reality will show that it comes as little surprise that Tina and Claire don't behave in the same way at all. They don't think the same way, so why would they act the same way?

They don't. When it comes to discretionary purchases, and plenty of non-discretionary purchases, the two buy vastly different products and services in vastly different ways. They may have grown up in the same house, but they live in different worlds. As a consumer – or, more to the point, a spender of money – Tina lives in a Finder's world. Claire lives in another. For example, Claire thinks brown eggs are ridiculous.

When Tina picked up that carton, she gave us a few behavioral clues. To begin with, Tina wasn't very interested in a brand name. A Finder does not use a brand as a measure of familiarity, trust, status, or any of the characteristics that are usually espoused by a brand. Instead, a Finder lives to discover the product itself on its own merits, for *herself*. Sure, there are brands that Tina would go for, but during any process of discovery she will seek markers for real authenticity. It would have done very little good for a big brand egg supplier to put the same eggs in those slightly grotty looking cartons. Tina would have seen beyond that. No, she wanted eggs that would connect her to the realness of the food. Real authenticity is an essential point of connection for the Finder. The words "organic" and "free range" mattered to Tina but not necessarily as political statements or even status markers. Like any Finder, she just wanted the "eggest" eggs she could find.

Now what about price? For a Finder who is making any kind of discretionary purchase, the product will always come before the price. To the Tinas of the world, the price is nothing more than another piece of information. In small purchases it is barely considered, and in larger purchases it stands as the exchange rate between two conditions – the condition of wanting and the condition of having.

Tina's egg purchase was by no means the one absolute that marked her as a Finder – it was a clue. To extend it a little further, the location for buying eggs, a supermarket, wasn't Tina's ideal for such a purchase either. Her ideal buy would have taken place right in front of the farmer at a market stall, or, for that matter, at the actual chicken coop. A Finder will go to some pretty spectacular lengths in the search for authenticity – as long as it's real authenticity. It is worth placing the word "real" in front of our use of the word "authenticity." It is used to isolate the conversation from the overused word "authenticity" in advertising, which has effectively rendered the word meaningless. Today it is that word that you are likely to see set against an ersatz Tuscan sunset and printed on the side of a frozen pizza box. "Authentic" has become the marketer's clumsy term brought into the advertising and packaging lexicon as a generalized reaction to growing suspicions of a market that they don't quite understand.

Age, gender, income, education, and marital status can tell us a few things. They can help local governments plan out the need for schools and hospitals, and they can let us calculate an approximate birth rate. Demographics can let us know how incomes are distributed along age, family, and gender lines. They just won't tell you very much about how that income will get spent. In this case, it's best that you get to know Tina. And Lloyd.

3

◆

CHEAPEST BY THE DOZEN

Meet the Keeper, the One Who Gets All the Attention

Lloyd and his shopping cart are on a bit of a roll. So far, Lloyd has found his favorite brand of peanut butter for $3 off, and his brand of cheese singles are exactly the same price as they are at Walmart. Paper towels are a good deal when he uses his wife's loyalty card, and now he's found a great Sunday-only deal on eggs. He might not really need a flat of twenty-four, but at this price, they'll keep.

Like Tina, this particular supermarket wasn't Lloyd's idea of the perfect store either but for a different set of reasons. The perfect store for Lloyd would hold a combination of the brands he knows and trusts, the lowest prices, and a wide variety of even lower prices on limited-time specials. In Lloyd's world, it is wise to give him the best deal. Otherwise Lloyd will be on his way to another place that will.

The Lloyds of this world are people who like to stick with what they trust. It is not that they hate to spend money it is just that their relationship with spending is far different from that of a Finder. For a guy like Lloyd, spending is about how much he will get for his money and how much of that money he will keep. Lloyd is a Keeper.

Keepers are a common sight and represent over 50 percent of the population. Yet, for all of their numbers they account for only 23 percent of discretionary spending. As the name suggests, they prefer to keep their money. Now do not splash 50 percent of the population with a pejorative term like cheapskate or skinflint. These people are not necessarily tight with their money nor are they poor. Keepers represent a broad spectrum of the population and include a large slice of the so-called one percent. Keepers simply hold a different and, by many definitions, more traditional outlook on the world. The word "traditional" is an interesting one. Let us bring it into context.

Tradition is by definition the transmission of customs and beliefs from generation to generation. Tradition then is a conduit to the past. For Keepers, the past is a very comfortable place. The past is where trusted brands come from. The past is a place where saving and keeping money is a respected virtue. Keepers like to keep things the way they were when the world felt more certain.

We have met the Finder and had a brief introduction to the Keeper. For the moment, that introduction will serve as a way of contrasting behaviors between these two very different kinds of spenders but before we take a deeper dive into what a Keeper is all about, let's return to the Finder's World.

4

◆

THIS LITTLE FINDER WENT TO MARKET

Shopping in a Finder's World

Last year Jessica bought a station wagon. She did not buy it for the status that might be attached to the brand name on it. In her case, brand didn't really enter into her thinking as much as what worked for her. She bought it for its solid build, its lower center of gravity, and its four-wheel-drive for runs up to the ski hill on winter weekends. She loves its roof racks that add capacity for skis, snowboards, mountain bikes, and paddleboards. The racks also come in handy for the long, rolled-up backdrops that she often uses in her job as a freelance photographer. Jessica likes the rubber-matted rear of the vehicle for her often soggy and dog-stinky trail-running buddy, Bob, her five-year-old, shelter rescued Labrador Retriever. With practicalities aside, Jessica loves the aesthetic of the car's long lines, its five-spoke mag style wheels, and its deep blue finish, even though the color loses a lot of luster when it's dirty, which it often is. It cleans up very nicely for the explorations that she and her husband take in search of great places to eat. She also considered its decent gas mileage over a Sport Utility Vehicle. Additionally, as a wagon, those often-used roof racks are a lot easier for her to reach. The car's 230 horsepower engine, six-speed transmission, and responsive handling offer some of the performance that she gave up when she traded in her hilariously fun but incredibly impractical Mini Cooper.

Like Tina, Jessica is a Finder. Her spending habits will consistently trend to lifestyle choices, aesthetics, and product quality over price. As a Finder, she is among those who are four times more likely to ski or snowboard than Keepers, twice as likely to surf or enjoy board sports, and 50 percent more likely to go for a run.

Her activities and attraction to aesthetic and performance led her to choose a car that scored on all of those levels. If you are guessing Subaru at this point, you might very well be correct but in this case, Jessica just wasn't into the look of those cars. If you are thinking that she went for a luxury brand, you would be half right, but it wasn't about the money.

Jessica has two kids in University and one in a semi-private high school. She is not an elitist; the kids attended a mix of private, high-performance sport schools and public schools. The choices were based on what she, her kids, and her husband felt best matched the individual child at pre-school, primary, middle, and high school levels. Right now, school is taking a sizable portion of Jessica's and her husband's incomes, even if those incomes are comfortably above average.

This meant that when it came to buying a new car Jessica had a mini-van-sized budget. But, she did not buy a mini-van or a small SUV or even a value-brand station wagon. If she had found one that fit her criteria she might have but instead she decided to trade the cost of new car depreciation for the cost of slower depreciation and the careful maintenance of a well-inspected used vehicle that will be kept under the watch of a trusted local mechanic. Jessica purchased the mix of everything that she wanted in a car (aesthetics, performance, and utility) and bought a five-year-old BMW sport wagon with all-wheel drive and 50,000 miles on the odometer. So far it has only been to the shop for scheduled maintenance. She is keeping her fingers crossed.

Right now that car and its owner are parallel parking on a busy street about a block away from an Italian grocer and butcher. On the shopping list today are some cheeses and sausages, olive oil, canned tomatoes, Tuscan bean soup, fresh basil, a few meats, her family's absolutely favorite free-range chicken, and lasagna that is made every Wednesday by the grocer's aunt using a closely held family recipe. Most of what she will buy will come with a bit of banter with the woman behind the counter. The two have been on a first-name basis for a few years now, ever since Jessica first walked in with a friend who married into an Italian family. She will also pick up some house-baked focaccia, a tiramisu, and a few bottles of Chianti before loading her cardboard box into the car and walking down the street to the green grocer. There, she will fill another box with primarily organic and locally farmed fresh vegetables and fruits. Some of this produce is actually grown on the small city lots of the Italian American pensioners who still proudly tend to their neat little backyard gardens.

If Jessica was getting fish today and had time to go to Chinatown, she might stop by the fishmonger's to select a live cod from the tank to be beheaded, cleaned and filleted on the spot and taken home on ice.

Instead, today's next stop is a Target store. It could be Walmart but Jessica has run out of her preferred cleaners for the sink and the bathroom. She buys this brand because it actually works well and does not contain a lot of noxious chemicals. She didn't have any luck finding it at Walmart – with its vast parking lot and friendly, greeter-attended sliding doors – on her last trip. Otherwise, toilet paper, bleach, light bulbs, dishwasher soap, and paper towels are the basic commodities that can be worth a trip to the bright lights and big checkout belts of any discount store that offers the lowest prices.

There is a point that ought to be made here. Jessica has a job, she has kids, and she does not lead a life of merry leisure. She could have bought near-facsimiles to most of those parallel-parking-required purchases during one stop at Walmart. She would have saved time and certainly money, but to Jessica the price difference means far less than the quality of what she is buying. And the time spent is actually part of what she sees innately as a key component of the actual quality of her life.

It's a joy for her to see the Italian grocer's familiar face in the store that offers the smells, sounds, accents, culture, family, and realness of Italy. Similar feelings are evoked for her because of the closeness to the farm in the produce store. Both represent a set of experiences and feelings that illuminate something that a Finder would happily trade for another activity: time. In a Finder's world time is meant to be spent well and not to be hoarded.

One can call time a currency that holds different values, or exchange rates if you will, in the worlds of Finders and Keepers. To a Finder, time spent discovering and experiencing while buying is part of the value that comes with the purchase. This stands in stark contrast to a Keeper's deeply ingrained point-of-view where the less time and the less money spent, the better the purchase.

Finders and Keepers don't travel through time at different speeds. There are all kinds of instances in a Finder's life where time is too much of a premium to allow for shopping that requires a lot of parking spot hunting, trips to different parts of town, and across-the-counter banter. However, even in those cases, a Finder will still avoid shopping like a Keeper. Instead, he or she will look for a central shopping destination that fits Finder values as closely as time allows. This is where we see the rise of what most mistakenly call "premium" or "upscale" grocery and retail. As far as it goes for those businesses, the standouts are those that align closely with Finder values.

Jessica didn't bother to look for a place that would be special to her when buying those items that do not hold any clear, discernable product quality differences from other products in the same category. Toilet paper, dishwasher detergent, and the like are commodities to her. Brands don't matter much to Jessica either.

When it comes to commodities, the only meaningful difference between products is price. Finders are not money wasters. If what they are buying isn't important to them – a commodity – they will buy like anyone else in the same circumstances and make their choices based on price.

Can't Buy Me Love

Let's review some constant Finder values that were revealed during Jessica's shopping trip as well as others that are common with Finders.

Sensory cues: These can include things like the tinkle of the bell upon entering the Italian grocer, or the feel of acceleration that her car delivers. Sensory cues are various and powerful. When a Finder goes shopping, the stores, brands, and products that can deliver on those senses, both conscious and unconscious, will align with them and profit from them.

Design: Jessica bought her car on function. Yet function could have been found in at least twenty other cars. Design was what tipped the scale. To her, the car's designers did a great job balancing all the function together with a clean and sleek shape. A poorly designed product, either aesthetically and/or functionally, will fail with the Finder. As Norton and Honeywill observe in their book, *One Hundred Thirteen Million Markets of One*, "Design shows you care."

Craftsmanship: Let's discuss another Finder's shopping experience. It could be a hand turned salad bowl crafted to last for at least a generation, or a perfectly tuned wheel on a precision built road bike. To truly understand the importance of craftsmanship, it helps to look at it as a transference and then storage of energy. Think of the energy exerted by expert hands in the sculpting of a handcrafted vase. It is as if the craftsman has transferred some of himself into that vase. The final finished product is more than just an output of work but a bit of the crafter's skill and energy stored in the object.

Invention: A multitude of product features don't necessarily equal invention. But take the simple example of the Philippe Starck juicer stand, a single, elegant, three-legged object invented to allow juice to be squeezed directly into a glass. In the case of this particular object, the design is as strong as the function for which it was invented.

Innovation: Invention's little brother, innovation is a thoughtful addition to established norms. Jessica likes the all-wheel drive system on her car. It isn't the first all-wheel drive system in the world but it is a smoother, seamless system that lets her car handle like a heavy but responsive sports sedan without being clunky. This could simply be looked on as a feature unless it deepens the user's enjoyment of the product. When it comes to innovation, Finders don't always need to be first, but they respect those brands and products that seek to be there for them.

Authenticity: That is, real authenticity, to be more accurate. Jessica found it in the Italian grocer. Finders seek it in what they eat, what they cook with, how they furnish their homes, and their travel destinations. Authentic isn't a brand, or a boast; it is simply the thing. It either is authentic or it isn't.

Provenance: Where did it come from? Who made it? What is its history? For example, the lasagna Jessica purchases is made from a recipe passed down through many generations.

Sharing: Jessica won't normally talk about what she spent during her shopping trips. However, Jessica will tell you about her favorite butcher, where to get fresh fish, and how the produce at the market is sourced from those local seniors in the neighborhood. Her shopping is an exploration of the stories behind what she buys. Sharing is the story of those stories.

5

◆

IT'S NOT ABOUT THE MONEY UNTIL IT'S ABOUT THE MONEY

You might already live in a Finder's world. You might even be one perhaps, depending on who you felt a kinship with in the egg purchasing scenario. Before you commit to seeing yourself as Finder or otherwise, there are a number of other qualities that we should explore that can illustrate the difference.

When it comes to what things cost, Finders are not stupid. You will have a hard time running into a Finder who is out to buy a gallon of gas that costs more – that is unless that Finder happens to be a car nut. The fact is Finders are cost sensitive in circumstances where what they are buying has no discernable difference from other products. These are the purchases that have low involvement, consumer products that are the same or similar across brands, or when the differences between brands and/or products are inconsequential to the Finder.

When a product is one that a Finder is completely dedicated to, say a favorite blend of coffee, there is an added stimulus to purchase if that coffee is on sale. Perhaps there is even a chance to achieve what the packaged goods people call, the act of pantry loading – stocking up. Yet there is an important distinction here:

if the product were not on sale, the Finder would have bought it anyway. For a Finder, cost is the <u>price</u> of what they want not the <u>creator</u> of what they want.

Frankie Goes to Costco

You might have recognized that some products are commodities to some people while not to others. In the case of a Finder, this is best illustrated by going shopping with one.

Frank's boots are made of deep brown leather with a motorcycle style heel made (since 1932) by Australian bootmaker, R.M. Williams. They are, in fact built to last longer than Frank himself. He thinks they're pretty great and he loves the comfort. It is a particular sort of comfort that he had to work for over what felt like a painfully long break-in period. He likes the sound the solid heels make when he walks on a hard surface. He likes that his wife likes them on him. The $400 price tag was steep but it was really only a bridge for him between wanting a great pair of boots and owning said boots. He gave it a little thought as he reached for his credit card but you will never hear him say, "Can you believe I paid four hundred bucks for these?!"

We are not here to talk about boots. We are here to talk about a big screen TV. Frank is buying one at a Costco warehouse store in Bellingham, Washington. He needs something with more than two HDMI slots for his Apple TV and his PVR, and a few USB slots for, well, he's not sure, but he heard they're good to have. He is not in the market for a wall-dominating monster; he wants one that is between 46" and 50". He read on the Internet that a fast refresh rate of 120 HZ is the way to go and 1080P means something good about sharpness – or something. To review: around 50", two HDMI, USB, 120HZ, 1080P. Now, as he cruises the valley of giant screens he sees a 50" Toshiba for $425. Then he comes across a Samsung at $395 and a Panasonic on sale at $355.

Frank thinks, "I can't see the difference and they all have what I want. I'm going for the deal." He tips one big cardboard Panasonic box into his giant cart and wheels toward the checkout with his kill.

You might be thinking, "Wait! One of those brands has better consumer ratings!" "Panasonic is the Plasma!" "Toshiba has a really good interface!" "I work for Samsung!" Frank doesn't care about those other factors. If he did, and for that matter if more people did, it is likely that we would all still be buying TVs from specialty stores instead of Costco. And if you need further proof, go ask Circuit City… oh wait, they went out of business.

What we have here is a case of a Finder not acting like a Finder. Finders like Frank will almost always show up and behave this way in purchases that carry little weight against the things that matter to them. These are the purchases and the products that can always be looked upon as commodities. This is particularly true when those products lack any clear differentiating qualities that really matter to buyers. For Finders and Keepers alike, the only thing that really matters with commodities is price.

Do not be fooled into thinking that only certain products can become commodities. Commodities are everywhere, growing fast, and what is considered a commodity is beginning to transcend the physical form and is appearing in service industries and increasingly becoming something that is represented by brand name.

Found

1. In the absence of anything meaningful to set one product apart from another, the only deciding factor in a Finder's purchase is price.

2. Which means that poorly differentiated products, brands, or categories cannot expect to profit to any greater extent from the purchases of Finders.

3. To hold any meaningful differentiating factors, product features and their attendant benefits must be relevant to the Finder or for that matter almost any buyer. If what's different doesn't matter to the person expected to pay for it, it's commodity time.

4. If it's only about price, Finders won't spend any more than they have to.

6

◆

THE FIELD GUIDE TO FINDERS

There are many business and consumption stories that can be told with a Finder at the center of it. Demographics generally measure on five metrics: Age, Education, Gender, Income, and Marital Status. Finders are far more multi-dimensional. To understand them, it is helpful to outline their defining characteristics in the following twenty-one points.

1. **Finders make purchases based on high levels of discretion instead of basic needs fulfillment.** Tina wasn't fulfilling a basic need for eggs, she was considering a set of key drivers that include the realness of the eggs (or real authenticity), the story behind them, and the particular pleasure she would get out of them.

2. **Finders are far more likely to spend.** Money is not the key driver. Pleasure is derived from discovery; therefore, the act of spending for a Finder is the act of discovering. They have an appetite for discovery, which leads to an appetite for spending.

3. **Finders earn more.** It takes money to be a Finder. That doesn't mean that all Finders are rich, or that being

rich makes you a Finder, it simply means that to be this good at spending, one must be equally skilled at earning. Norton and Honeywill report that NEOs (Finders) are five times more likely than average to earn over $100,000 per year.

4. **Brands do not work the same way with Finders.** The traditional role of a brand is to act as a promise of the qualities, properties, and even personality of a product. To many, and to Keepers like Lloyd in particular, a brand can be purchased and used to help symbolize the status, values, and character of that particular consumer. Finders travel in the opposite direction seeking products that can be treated as inside information among those with the same values. The values of the company that makes the product, the quality, and real authenticity matter far more than the brand. Brands only matter to the Finder when they connect with their values and are a unique mental shortcut to what is actually different and special about the product that the brand represents.

5. **Finders are masters of their own universe.** Finders are individualists and believe that they make their own way in the world powered by their own talents, skills, and planning. They believe far more in self-determination than following tradition and authority.

6. **Finders love the story.** Where it came from, what it's about, how it's made, who made it or created it – the

provenance of the product is key. Finders have a huge appetite for real and rich information, not hyperbole. They will read more and look for more. The more interesting and insightful the information they can absorb around a product, the more value it has to them.

7.   **Finders spend money and Finders spend time.** To Finders, time is a different currency. The idea of "saving time and money" only applies to buying uninteresting commodities. Otherwise, it just doesn't make sense. Part of the value that the purchase contains is the time spent going to that special place, examining the qualities of a purchase, or learning its story.

8.   **Finders find. They will try something new first.** They will not do this to be "the first kid on the block" as a symbol of status. Instead they seek adventure in discovery of the new and the sense of individuality that comes with being a pioneer in adopting something different.

9.   **Finders seek the real authentic.** Craftsmanship, passion, the feel of handmade, and real mastery matters and is as important to them when they shop for clothing, vacations, or furniture as it is when they order a burger in a pub. Finders seek real authenticity and have excellent radar for rejecting artificial claims made to further a sale.

10.   **A good deal is something that will be worth more after it is bought.** A Finder will desire an object that improves with age, use, or the pleasure of ownership. Imagine an

object as simple as a coffee mug turned by a master potter and bought from that very artisan at a market. It could be a copper cooktop hood that develops a patina, or boots, like Frank's, that will look and feel great once broken in. In each case, a Finder is looking for things that will either physically improve or provide ongoing or increased pleasure with continued ownership. This "worth-more-later" attraction is a phenomenon among Finders that spans everything from construction jackets to furniture.

11. **Finders don't trust discounts.** Not even the most dyed-in-the-wool Finder wants to pay more, yet a Finder will not look at a discount or price offer as the primary reason to buy. There must be variables in place beyond price before any discount makes sense to them. Sure, they will buy their favorite shirt for 40% off, but the important distinction is that it must be the exact favorite. Anything else is just an unhappy compromise.

12. **For Finders, product and experience come before price.** Price is no more than the bridge between desire and ownership.

13. **Price only matters when a Finder doesn't really care about the product.** A gallon of gas is a gallon of gas. Anything that doesn't strike a desire in the Finder will be treated the same way as any other commodity and price will be foremost.

14. **Their first instinct is to look for the best and spend accordingly.** Finders will look for the best quality first which makes them willing to spend at the top price points in almost every product category.

15. **Eating is much more than sustenance.** Food and beverage enjoyment and consumption is a constant frontier of exploration and discovery.

16. **Finders are tribal.** Once a Finder discovers something new he or she will almost literally "bring it back to the tribe" by sharing that discovery through word of mouth, or through social media with friends and those who share the same values. They have a strong sense of social, environmental, community, and ethical responsibility and seek to gather consensus around their opinions. Finders will tend to lead thought rather than follow doctrine.

17. **Finders are leading edge.** They are always the first to adopt new technologies and remain the heaviest users of the Internet. They are reluctant to accept second-best when it comes to technology and therefore act as drivers to the premium-priced category in consumer technology innovations.

18. **Finders are all ages.** Finders can be found in most age brackets but are more highly represented with those between their late twenties and their late forties.

19. **Mass marketing tends to miss Finders.** Their preference is to engage with true relationship marketing where the seller has a clear take on the individual and allows the Finder to set the terms of the relationship.

20. **Finders are gluttons for information.** Finders want to go deep so magazines, with their specialized content, emphasis on design, and leading edge trend reporting still figure in their information consumption habits. Their willingness to pay for quality content increases their propensity to subscribe to specialty cable TV. They are medium viewers of commercial television.

21. **Finders are elastic in their careers.** A strong appetite for learning and personal development, the search for the new, and a hunger for information are all traits that transcend mere consumption among Finders and drive them toward increased mobility and exploration in their careers. Individualism and less of an adherence to playing by conventional rules means a strong entrepreneurial streak among Finders.

7

THE COMMODITY TRAP

It's All the Same to Them

There are products, services, and experiences that can only be viewed as commodities in both the Finder's and the Keeper's worlds. In the general sense, these are products that cannot or will not be different. At the most basic level these are goods such as non-organic all purpose flour, bottled water, refined sugar, salt, or gasoline. In these cases, brand and price might be the only differentiator.

Points of difference are generally associated with a brand. Some of these are real, discernable, and demonstrable differences such as the long, slow pour of Heinz Ketchup that built decades worth of advertising campaigns. (Interestingly, Heinz dropped this point once it realized it could sell more ketchup with a squeeze bottle.) Others are invented and abstract perceptions such as Nike's once ubiquitous "Just Do It" campaign that associated the brand and, consequently, the buyer as an active, inspiring, and high performing entity.

This brings the idea of a branded commodity into an interesting place and raises a question. If a high value consumer who comes in the form of a Finder rejects a brand name, can a brand name simply become an identifier for a commodity?

Four Kinds of Commodities:

1. The Basics: No actual difference between products. These include such things as gasoline, all purpose flour, white sugar, table salt, aluminum foil, and printer paper.

2. Dominant brands: Where a brand has so much market share that it defines that market to the extent that it is one-of-a-kind leaving that brand in a place where the only way to stimulate further sales is to create price reductions or short term promotions. It is hard to sympathize with a market-share-gobbling brand such as Heinz Ketchup but, for a brand manager, there are few places to travel to beyond short-term sales gains.

3. Brands and competitive brands where perceptible differences have been erased by "me too" products. Once it was Kleenex, Saran Wrap, Windex, and Xerox. These are brand names that once doubled for a category's description. Now they're names that have run full circle to the generic descriptions known today as Tissue, Plastic Wrap, Window Cleaner, and Photocopier.

4. Technological parity products: These include generic technologies such as second and even first tier brand flat screen televisions, mobile phones, and digital cameras where there are no meaningful, stand-alone innovations that set them apart from other brands.

Finally, we arrive at the real definition of commodity versus non-commodity with this definition:

A product is not a commodity as long as it is clearly different in ways that its buyer really cares about.

8

◆

LET'S MAKE A DEAL

Shopping with a Keeper

It's 8:30 on a Saturday morning as Sandra slides her McDonald's coffee into the cup holder of her new Chevrolet Traverse. She loves this vehicle. First, there's the fact that she can fit her three kids with their sports gear and friends. It has eight seats and best-in-class 116.3 cubic feet of cargo space. She feels the six passenger airbags are great, so is the touch screen radio thingee. It has a sunroof, forward collision alert, lane departure warning, and a 5-year/100,000 mile powertrain warranty. Here's what sealed the deal. Not only did she save $4,000, she still hasn't paid a penny for it! It came with a limited time, do-not-pay-for-90-days offer that means she won't have to drop a cent for almost three months. And, by taking the one on the lot, she got it four weeks ahead of the usual order delivery time and the dealer threw in a full set of rubberized floor mats worth over $400. Sandra would have preferred it in red but she's getting used to its color even though she's not crazy about beige. It's really not beige anyway – it's champagne silver metallic.

Sandra is off to an early start today; later she'll be attending Girl Guides with her youngest and catching her son's afternoon soccer game. Tonight's plans include a video and maybe a glass or two of Robert Mondavi while her husband knocks back a few cans of Coors Light.

Sandra rightly considers herself to be a little more than a smart shopper; she's a bit of a genius. With this week's flyer in hand, she's on her way to get the shopping done and dusted. Later she'll be dropping off the groceries and picking up one of the kids. There's a sale on at TJ Max and Sandra needs a new pair of jeans. Her youngest daughter is looking for back to school clothes. This will get taken care of today and by-God they are going to hang on to their money and keep as much of it as they can because, after all, Sandra is a Keeper.

First it'll be the groceries at Walmart. She'll stop by the frozen foods section because there's a deal on Marie Callender's frozen lasagna. She puts one in her cart and turns to the frozen vegetables where she grabs two bags of Green Giant steamers. Then it's on to the cereal aisle for Quaker instant oatmeal and Post Great Grains at $3.72 a box. Next is Starkist tuna at $2.48 a can. She keeps a loose running total as her cart quickly fills with trusted brands at great prices. In the meat aisle, Tyson trimmed and ready chicken breasts are on sale. In they go and that'll be what's on the menu tonight – that is until she spies a great deal on Farmland pork spareribs. Ribs should be a reward for today's shopping and at two for one, ribs it is.

Sandra rolls on through the paper goods section until she spots the warehouse deal on toilet paper. It balances precariously atop her fast-filling cart. As she passes the in-store McDonald's, Sandra glances down at the now empty drive-thru McDonald's coffee cup balanced in the cart's cup holder and wonders if they offer free refills. She doesn't act on this thought but considers it an interesting conversation piece to file away in her rich storehouse of "deal savvy" that sits somewhere in a cluster of well developed neurons in her brain.

She's a fairly active and energetic woman, but lately Sandra has been putting more thought into her health. This means one more stop in the vitamin and supplement section. She can hear the voice of Dr. Oz in her head. He recommends that every woman over thirty-five take a multivitamin every day including A, all the Bs, C, D, and E. According to him, calcium is important for bone health in women. Then there's magnesium to help her body process the calcium and Omega 3 as an important supplement for mental clarity and stress management. He also says that taking these properly twice a day will help keep you young. Vitamins are expensive. Sandra spends quite a lot of time considering her options and prices. She's getting impatient but she has to do this for herself, and Dr. Oz's compassionate voice of authority is practically ringing in her ears. She calculates prices using the calculator that came on her Samsung smartphone. She does some quick passes and decides on the best deals based on number of dosages per package and corresponding price. On another day she might have shopped around and done more research on the best deals, but today she feels like she did the right thing.

Now she'll power that carefully planned cart toward the long checkout lines by way of the bedding and housewares section. It's there where she will do one quick price check on cotton sheets. All of her sheet sets are getting a little threadbare and pilled so that puts her in the market for a new set. She will wait to see when they're a great deal. Who knows, she might find them at TJ Max today but wants to be prepared by setting a baseline price that will be accomplished with a quick glance at some comparable sets that could be on sale here today.

Now it's through the checkout, a quick review of the bill and back out to the SUV. Sandra delights as the automatic tailgate opens at the push of a button on her key fob. "Just like an Escalade," she thinks to herself.

In her shopping today, Sandra spent the currency of time as carefully as she did her money. In her world, time is something to be spent on anything but everyday shopping, unless that shopping comes with a reward in the form of an extraordinary deal. Then it's worth it.

Remember Jessica and her trip to the Italian grocer? Sandra might very well step into Jessica's territory from time to time but the two will never fully occupy each other's worlds. Sandra might very well enter that very same Italian grocer filled with sounds, sights, and smells of a world created in the likeness of the owner's family memories and values. The place would likely delight

Sandra with the sort of thrill that a traveler feels when entering a distant land but, as a consumer far from her own world, thoughts would return to home, a place where shopping reverts to time and money saved. As much as what Jessica does is part of her, what Sandra does as a consumer will always be a part of her and will carry a different outlook on any purchase she might make in that enclave of Italian food culture. What she would be doing there is what marketing-speak will generalize as "premium purchasing." This definition can be forgiven. Its point of view is too often formed through the lens that sees too much of a world populated by Keepers.

For Sandra, that homemade lasagna from said Italian grocer would be considered something of an exotic purchase; it would be enjoyed as a special meal from a special place. Sandra would savor the handmade pasta and secret family sauce from a generations-old recipe. She might notice the ricotta cheese and the fresh mozzarella as it melts in her mouth with a creaminess that perfectly offsets the spice and savory bite of lamb, pork, beef, Italian sausage, and fresh herbs. Yet Sandra would also live in another kind of enjoyment, one that would probably never appear with Jessica. It would be a kind of satisfaction that would come from an entirely different place in Sandra's being – the same region of her mind where the possibility of that free McDonald's coffee refill is kept. What Sandra's mind would touch on is the thought that this lasagna is a special treat that she paid a lot more for. The lasagna then contains a monetary unit of measurement that to Sandra acts as evidence of its quality. Sandra paid what is commonly called a premium price for a premium quality product to be enjoyed as a premium experience. For Keepers like Sandra, when it comes to consumption, everything finds its true north around one thing: price.

Can Buy Me Love

Sensory Cues: Sandra might have a sixth sense called the deal detector. In contrast to those of a Finder, sensory cues for a Keeper are less what they might call esoteric, and more what they would call direct. A Keeper is a short-term information seeker. "Tell me the price and I'll be on my way, thanks."

Features: Sandra loved all the stuff that came on her car. None of those features were particularly new or inventive but were just-new-enough-to-matter features that added up to more value in the purchase.

Status: There was a hint at Cadillac. It demonstrates how a status symbol brand can be used to transfer and project that brand's status to the owner and, accordingly, that person's place in the world, which brings us to…

Brand: The etymology of Brand actually comes from the branding iron that has been used on cattle since, presumably, the invention of steak. Sandra used brands as shorthand for assurance of quality in her purchases. Brands let Sandra identify a constant against which she can measure value. She knows what to expect in that Robert Mondavi wine and those Quaker

Oats. To a Keeper the brand is the constant. The variable is what it might be on sale for.

Discount: A discount means a deal – an opportunity for a Keeper to keep.

Immediacy: She went for the ribs. Faced with something on sale for a limited time she will change plans.

Security and Ubiquity: Sandra will go with what she trusts. She wouldn't exactly be going out on a limb by buying coffee almost anywhere else but there is certain strength in numbers for a Keeper by the ubiquity of, for example, 35,000 McDonald's locations pouring coffee worldwide.

Reward: Loyalty programs can be seen as collectable discounts and are another type of reward. Furthermore, an upgrade or a club member discount can also carry a measure of status.

Newness was a turn off: Few understand the premium for getting the latest technology better than a Keeper like Sandra. She might adopt the iPhone at the right price but is perfectly happy and even proud to own "second-in" technology with her Samsung. Sandra thinks that anyone who would line up all night to pay huge bucks for the latest "iThing" is silly. It is worth giving Samsung some credit at this point for understanding its Keeper faithful. In a commercial timed to go with the September 2012 launch of the iPhone 5, the brand quite effectively and hilariously lampooned those "weirdos" lined up for their dose of Apple's latest leading-edge gadget.

Sharing: When you hear someone declare, "Can you believe the deal I got on this thing?" chances are that someone is a Keeper. If you're looking for a deal, stay close and listen carefully; knowledge of the best deals can be something of a calling card among the most developed of Keepers.

Keepers can be seen to behave in the same way as Finders under certain circumstances, but they will never move into their world. From a consumption standpoint, the Keeper's world is one that contains many of the commodities that both Finders and Keepers need and use. This makes it easy to assume that Finders can behave as Keepers. This is always a temporary condition. The opposite is less true, a Keeper will rarely behave as a Finder even when found in a Finder's world. Their visits are still based on a monetary exchange.

9

◆

A KEEPER IN KEEPER'S CLOTHING

There are Finders in Keeper's clothing. On the other hand, it is a little harder to spot Keepers engaging in that same kind of role reversal. More can be learned by going on one more shopping trip with a Keeper while he does what Keepers do.

It has been a long time in the making but today is a good day for Gary as he celebrates a victory in the parking lot outside his fourth electronics store since breakfast. Gary has done his research, checked the flyers and online discounts, the warehouse stores, and the clearance centers and finally has it. "It" is THE DEAL: A Sony 3D HDTV with WIFI connectivity, three HDMI ports, and built-in simulated surround sound. If he's honest, Gary will not use most of these features but he will use the extra set of free 3D glasses that came with it. Then there's the sound bar that was free as a today-only bonus. This isn't just any TV. It is a Sony. So in a small way the Sony brand now speaks of a Gary who appreciates and can own something a little better. It is a TV that comes with more features than almost anything on the market. The sound bar gets pretty close to a full surround system. The cost? Sound bar and all plus a free HDMI cable; for $780. This is a TV that first came out two years ago at a suggested retail price of nearly two grand. That $780 price is guaranteed by the store to be the best price on that model of Sony against any competitor for ninety days. Gary's feeling righteously resourceful and he feels pretty good about his status as a member of the Sony owning family. He wrestles the big, awkward flat screen TV box into the back seat of his car and heads for home. Gary is one happy Keeper.

No one can argue with the wisdom of this purchase. It was, after all, one heck of a deal; it was enough of a deal to stimulate the day's activity. Without it, Gary's shopping might not have been worth the trip. At anything close to full retail price, it wouldn't have happened at all.

There are a number of key behaviors that Gary has shown us in this demonstration. First, a brand name is an important piece of information to a Keeper. This brand signals status and on a deeper level helps to define the character of the owner. Gary can now see himself as a "Sony guy." Secondly, the more features the product comes with, the better. Features work to bring a sense of volume and extra abundance to the product. Then there is the immediacy of "today only" which brought a sense of a special moment to the deal before linking with yet another added value in the form of that free sound bar. This combination of a limited-time promotion and an added premium delivered more stimulants to the bundle of "the deal." Finally, and most importantly, there was the price. The sale price and margin between the original retail price was the most tangible part of the joy of buying that our Keeper experienced.

There was little attention paid to the fact that this particular TV costs less today than it did two years ago. In our world of overnight technological obsolescence, it is selling for less because, logically, it is worth less. This in the mind of a Keeper is somewhat irrelevant. Instead, there is a level of honorability that comes with buying that older model at a much lower price. After all, "Good things come to those who wait."

The Parable of the Lazy Little Squirrel

You may have heard this one. It is a tale where a squirrel refuses to gather nuts in preparation for a long cold winter. Soon his anti-establishment behavior gets him the kind of girlfriend who goes for that kind of thing. So, instead of hunting down a winter's store, the two frolic and play happily secure in the assumption that their boring, hoarding-obsessed neighbors will share from their undoubtedly deep stocks once the snow begins to fly.

The frost sets in and with it comes a heaping helping of bad news. Cold and hungry, our two nitwits are informed by the wise and just Head Squirrel that, by taking a share of the bounty, they would endanger the whole community. And, by the way, tough acorns. Everyone smiles and waves as the two are politely kicked out into the frozen forest for what we can assume to be a cute, furry doom.

One might think this is a satisfying ending, particularly if one happens to be a Keeper. Not to say that Keepers are humorless sadists – far from it. Keepers tend to be honest and moral people. And this story has a moral – one that teaches every good squirrel to work hard, think ahead, and prepare. One cannot deny its lesson. There is a subtext here that resonates more deeply with Keepers than it would with Finders. Make no mistake, those lazy, fun loving squirrels are NOT Finders. They're just naïve and dumb squirrels. But the images of safety represented by abundance and authority strike a note with Keepers. That Head Squirrel, the parable's definition of authority, is one who speaks with wisdom, nobility, and integrity and who brings structure and safety to the humble hard-working background players in this story. Keepers tend to identify with this sort of positive and protective authority. Then there are those hard-won and well-stored nuts. Keepers enjoy a sense of feeling protected by the presence of plenty. There is the satisfaction of getting as much as possible for their labors. In spending, Keepers behave very much in this way; they seek to gather as much around themselves as they can. This drives their strong relationship with getting a deal. Even though on the surface a deal might be about getting more for less, it goes deeper. A deal means security and self-validation, a reward for hard work and resourcefulness. In this way The Parable of the Lazy Squirrel is, in its inverse, the Parable of the Honest Keeper.

◆

10

THE SPOTTER'S GUIDE TO THE GREAT AMERICAN KEEPER

As well understood as they might seem, Keepers display more dimensions than common demographics could describe. Here they are, measured, identified, and preserved in sixteen points.

1. **Keepers are low activity discretionary spenders.** They will make discretionary purchases but must be highly stimulated before doing so.

2. **Keepers represent a slim majority of the population but spend in the minority.** At just over 50 percent of the population, their proportion of discretionary spending falls far behind at around 23 percent.

3. **Keepers keep.** They don't like to spend, have less to spend, or simply will not spend therefore will consume very lightly.

4. **Cost comes first, features second, status third; everything else comes last.** Functions and features matter more than design. Keepers will count up the amount of features and functions in any consumer good and balance that against the cost. Quality, craftsmanship,

and design matter far less than cost and features. Cost is always first.

5. **Keepers are event buyers.** Short-term sales, limited-time offers, one-day sales, door-crashers, and special offers are the bait that get Keepers biting.

6. **Time is Money.** Time is a currency to be kept almost as carefully as money; if there is a deal to be struck, time is worth spending. To a Keeper, in cases where the deal is a given, the less time and the less money, the better the purchase.

7. **Brands are assurance.** The values advertised, promoted, and communicated through a brand are touchstones to trust. They symbolize a sense of safety to a Keeper. Keepers will often accept a trusted brand over the actual quality of the product that it represents. This is an opposite behavior to that of a Finder.

8. **Brands are biographical.** The logo on the shirt, the coffee cup, the wristwatch, or the car is a symbol of who a given Keeper is, his or her place in the world, and what that Keeper does. This is something of a paradox in that it shows those who consume less as more conspicuous in their consumption.

9. **Keepers are traditionalists.** They will trust something that is tried and true and avoid or reject the new and innovative. Innovative to a Keeper can be another word for trendy. That word to a Keeper is seldom a compliment.

10. **Money does not change Keepers.** Wealthy Keepers remain infrequent buyers and are still motivated by the same drivers as any other Keeper: price, features, and status.

11. **Wealthy Keepers are more conspicuous.** Like their less moneyed brethren, wealthy Keepers are conspicuous consumers with the volume turned up to eleven. They will buy high status premium brands as symbols of their success.

12. **Keepers are more aligned with authority.** Keepers are less likely to have a strong sense of self-determination. They are more likely to look at life as something that is determined by authority, a higher power, or just luck. Keepers are less likely to see their own actions as a determination of their destiny.

13. **Keepers are late technology adopters.** As use of the Internet becomes ubiquitous, Keepers can still be seen as arriving late to the party in terms of search usage, social media, online shopping, and the purchase of leading edge mobile devices.

14. **Keepers are every age.** You will find a Keeper in every age group but they are more highly represented in the fifty plus category.

15. **Keepers are members.** Keepers are more likely to belong to a club or an organization with its attendant policies

and traditions than the more individualistic Finder who will tend to form a loose tribe around less organized but shared interests.

16. **Keepers make better mass communication target markets.** Keepers carry a preference for the assurance of mass advertising and marketing over more individualized communication.

11

◆

KEEP THE MONEY ROLLING IN AND KEEP THE MONEY

The High Status Keeper

It would be naïve to say that there are no socio-economic divisions between Finders and Keepers but those divisions are not nearly as great as one might think. Remember the lower income sub set of Finders? An Evolving Finder won't have the budget to choose a boutique hotel or an electric car but, with exactly the same income as any Keeper, that Evolving Finder will still behave differently. He will still look at quality before price; he will still search for provenance in a discretionary purchase. It is, for example, far more likely that he will shop for a used but interesting dinette set on Craigslist over a new pressboard and laminate pub style set on sale for $299 at Big Lots.

From there you can go to the opposite end of the socio-economic spectrum and find one of the most interesting constants between Finders and Keepers – one that will surface when a Keeper has a lot of money. Called a High Status Keeper, he will buy more, spend more, and do more than the average Keeper but will always follow Keeper patterns.

Similarly, a high income Finder will follow high-income Finder patterns; he or she will do more Finding.

It's just another case of differences between Finders and Keepers, only one that comes with a giant gold plated hi-liter run through it. High Status Keepers are about the price on both ends. They will purchase a valuable object in order to talk about, or simply display it as a marker of monetary success. This activity will be supported with the usual Keeper-style attention to getting the lowest price but, once that is done, the High Status Keeper will advertise ownership by wearing or owning it as a figurative personal price tag. Keepers use a brand as a talisman to reflect and broadcast its particular attributes as a partial description of their own personal place in the world. High Status Keepers go one step further by owning status symbols that give them, instead of a "brand-before person" level of recognition, a "price-before person" identity.

Show and Keep

There are two parts to the High Status Keeper transaction. First, there is the part where that High Status Keeper will work to save money (keep) during a high-value purchase; second there is the after-purchase phase where the High Status Keeper will "show." The two elements have a tendency to run together.

Alan is the CEO of a mortgage finance company. He is a hard-working guy who has come a long way in this world from humble beginnings, Alan is a fun, nice guy. He has plenty of good stories and is up for anything. He's a great guy to spend an afternoon with on the golf course, and he's the sort of person who gets invited to a lot of parties. It is at one of those parties that you could get a look at a sparkling symbol of "Alan-ness" that adorns the wrist of his lovely wife. For the past six months, a standard part of her party wear has been a spectacular diamond bracelet, or, to be more accurate, an it-won't-be-long-until-these-are-real-diamonds bracelet. It certainly looks like the real thing. It isn't. Not yet. For now it is set with a cluster of the finest cubic zirconia. Alan bought his wife this particular showpiece at a discount diamond warehouse, one that guarantees the very lowest price on diamonds. The purchase process is pretty simple. Choose the setting, order the diamonds, at the lowest possible price – lowest indeed on the market, and wait for the diamonds to arrive a few months later. In the meantime, a temporary piece set in simulated diamonds is loaned. Last Christmas season, when the party time of year was in full swing, Alan presented his wife with this bracelet, much to her delight. The two traveled from party to party, while onlookers admired what hung from her wrist, a triumphant symbol of Alan's hard work and achievement. Her wrist came in handy; his was busy supporting a Rolex. In a Keeper's world, Alan has done a great thing. He has negotiated for, and captured as much diamond bracelet as money can buy. The wisdom of his purchase reflects part of the financial acumen that has taken him such a long way in his very successful life. This specific purchase allows him to publicly broadcast his achievements. Soon the real diamonds will arrive and, shortly after that, another party season will come along where the couple will travel the circuit with the bracelet on full display.

It is said that there are things in life that you can't put a price on. Some even say that you can't put a price on success. But, in the case of the High Status Keeper, you can put a price on the successful.

12

◆

THE GREAT KEEPER OVERPOPULATION DECEPTION

The One Fish in the Sea Theory

The absence often in deep research and, oddly, in the presence of their own experience, marketers can tend to overstate the importance of Keepers to the frightening extent that they can fall into a trap of seeing Keepers as representative of the population as a whole.

Why? Maybe it's because in many ways too many of us are still fishing.

Imagine that you are a fisherman working a particular piece of the sea using one kind of bait. Every time you use that bait you catch fish. It works every time. These are good times and you keep pulling up the same species of fish. You get to thinking that these are the only fish in that ocean; after all, up here on the surface they're all you see. You might imagine a few other kinds, but really who cares when the fishing is easy and the rewards are plentiful.

Another boat pulls up. It uses the same bait, only a little more of it. It's a bigger boat that can fish with more lines. It isn't long before your catch starts to get a little lighter while at the same time you need more and more bait to attract those fish. Eventually, you're spending more on bait than what you're getting from that deep, mysterious water.

Meanwhile, other fishers are using the same bait in competition for those fish. And they're going to China to get it. And they're saving on bait.

You are not totally blind to what is going on under the surface. You have some fish finding gear and a bit of underwater observation equipment. You could call it market research.

You discover that there are other fish, big fish, that don't often go for your bait. They might not even go for any bait at all. You try to go after them with louder bait, bait with special features and incentives. It doesn't work. You see them but you just can't catch them. You only know how to catch Keeper fish.

It is only natural to overstate the importance of the Keeper because Keepers have always responded to the easiest bait for businesses to come up with: The Deal. When we provide the deal, customers come and we begin to define, what is really only a segment of customers, as all of the customers.

The Hazards of Keeper Fishing

It would be enough if Keepers were just attracted to the deal. They are not. They are attracted to the biggest deal. This is a problem because something needs to give when a business is trapped in a downward race toward the lowest price and, correspondingly, the pursuit of the lowest cost. In that race, there are two primary casualties: quality and profitability.

Returning to the nautical theme here and to paraphrase Roy Scheider in Jaws, you're not going to need a bigger boat, you're going to need an entirely different kind of boat. When it comes to the biggest boat, someone else already has it. Ahoy, there it is, the world's largest company and the world's biggest boat. The good ship Walmart.

If your company is not Walmart and you only see an ocean of Keepers out there, you'll need to get used to this jaunty nautical tune, "If you don't have the biggest boat, you're sunk".

Keepers are an excellent source of business for the right businesses – the ones that know how to fish for Keepers better than anyone else. Yet a dependence on Keepers and, even worse, a fixation on Keepers as the only kind of consumer in the sea, has meant the end of many businesses. You can get a very good perspective on this when you look at how the last recession left many overturned fishing boats bobbing on the Sea of Bankruptcy. Could they have been saved? Yes and no. But given the recession-proof quality of Finder focused businesses, those very failures tell their own tales.

13

◆

EVOLVING FINDERS

The Kids Are All Right

Jason is twenty-three and a recent graduate of Pratt Institute's Engineering program in New York. Demographically speaking, Jason is a millennial Like many of his millennial contemporaries, he is getting around to thinking about what he'll be doing with his life. Right now, he's more of an artisan than an engineer working as a TIG welder in a workshop housed in the sprawling factory complex that used to service the U.S. Navy's Atlantic fleet. At its peak, during World War II, the yard employed upwards of 70,000 welders, shipwrights, and, presumably, more than a few Rosie the Riveters. This is the same complex that is now filling up with cottage industries that are crafting, designing, and hand-making everything from high-end bags made from recycled seatbelts to architectural fabrication shops. Meanwhile, three time zones away in San Francisco, in an until recently disused garment workshop located across the street from the long-closed Levis Strauss Factory, another guy like Jason is, quite ironically, designing and producing jeans that sell for $300 a pair. Our Brooklyn Jason doesn't make the kind of money that enables him to wear $300 jeans, but he's happy with his thrift-store jacket – a Carhart that should, at least technically, last him the rest of his natural life. Jason went for an incredibly high quality garment. If it could talk it could tell you a story or two from the abrasions, tears, and burns that have taken up residence on its faded, heavy-duty, twelve-ounce, black duck cotton. Apart from that, it's just a really good jacket that was priced at less than the forty bucks he had in his wallet.

When Jason goes for a beer after work today he won't be calling it Miller time, he will be going to one of the neighborhood's flourishing brewpubs. And while we're on the subject of liquids, it is worth mentioning that Jason didn't go to a Dunkin Donuts for a coffee this morning. He stopped in to Brooklyn Coffee Roasters.

You can call Jason a millennial and you may have already called him a Hipster. Your description might even be absolutely accurate, but long after he shaves the beard that you're imagining and loses the black frame glasses that form your mental picture, he will get himself his dream job at a battery technology company and from there on and forever more Jason will be a Finder. Right now, he's an Evolving Finder.

This is important: Finders and Evolving Finders are individuals and, to that point, Jason is not representative of a whole set. You will discover Evolving Finders in all manner of industries, jobs, and sets of interests. Indeed a large segment of Evolving Finders are millennials but you will also find them across all demographics. Their identifying characteristics are a set of values and attitudes that align more closely with Finders: a sense of self-determination, a different relationship with big brands and big marketing, and even at a lower budget level, a product-before-price way of consuming.

Jason could have afforded a jacket from Walmart for under $40 but he would not have had the jacket he wanted. So he went out and found it in a completely different way. Jason could also afford twice as many cups of 7-Eleven or Dunkin Donuts coffee when compared to the house roasted coffee that he had this morning. But, even with this small purchase, quality and product are well ahead of price. Evolving Finders make the same choices as Finders when they have elasticity in their budgets to afford them. But when they can't, even more interesting things happen.

Let's call it "creativity as a survival instinct" or maybe even "creativity as an evolutionary ace up the sleeve."

Creativity Versus the Angry Bear

A caveman is out picking berries on a damp prehistoric springtime afternoon. Suddenly he comes upon a mother bear. He begins to back away quietly while recalling the common caveman rules of bear escape. While engrossed with that short mental list, he backs into a small bear cub and steps on its foot. The cub cries out in protest. Mother Bear rears up in ursine-style maternal consternation. The now possibly-soon-to-be-dead caveman looks around in the fervent hope of a nearby tree to climb. No tree. He looks for a big bear-discouraging rock to throw. No rock. In desperation he pulls two bushes out of the soft earth, holds them over his head until the combined size of caveman and bushes seem to dwarf the mother bear. He backs away in what he considers to be a large bearish manner while roaring his best big bear imitation in as loud a voice as he can. She gives a giant hairy shrug, a basso profundo dismissive grunt, and returns to the berries. He escapes. There we have it, a demonstration of creativity at work as a survival instinct so powerful that it can be considered part of human evolution. After all, our caveman can now live on to presumably pick more berries and perhaps father equally if not even more resourceful cave children.

With the Evolving Finder, a lack of money (rocks, or trees to climb) creates a level of creativity and resourcefulness that in turn forces someone who is attracted to the aesthetic and the individualistic to behave in different and resourceful ways.

It is exactly the creativity and resourcefulness created by a lack of excess funds that is driving Evolvers to power emerging, game changing, and extremely fast growing business models. Airbnb is an excellent example of this phenomenon. The website, founded in August 2008, allows people to rent out lodgings in their homes and in turn provide rental accommodations worldwide. Airbnb has over 1,000,000 listings in 34,000 cities and 192 countries worldwide. Its combination of adventure, individualized choices, and affordability for those who want to travel in their own ways and on their own terms (often budgetary) has created a company that now threatens the established hospitality industry and is the poster child for what is now being called the sharing economy.

Call them hipsters. Laugh at their funny hats and ratty beards, but a longing for something better than a crappy cup of coffee or watery beer with a big brand label is putting Evolving Finders on a mission to find, frequent, or create better things for everybody who wants them. Even those who don't know they want them. Yet.

14

◆

THE ANATOMY OF AN EVOLVING FINDER

1. **Evolving Finders are Finders on a budget.** They hold very similar values in areas that don't involve consumption and would hold almost the exact same values around purchasing as full-fledged Finders if they were in the same financial position.

2. **Evolving Finders are conflicted.** An Evolving Finder is often forced by financial limitations to shop like a Keeper and settle for inferior quality based on price.

3. **Evolving Finders are resourceful.** They will take their search for quality on a different path than that of a Finder by going where a Finder might not. That might mean everything from browsing thrift stores to using online shopping resources such as Craigslist, eBay, and Amazon to find the quality that they seek at a price they can afford.

4. **Evolving Finders are creating a new world.** While Finders define the richest market now, the resourceful drive found within Evolving Finders takes the

adventurous and individualistic qualities of Finders and builds in a search for affordability. This is creating revolutions in lower cost, high quality purchases such as craft beers and coffees. Yet even more profoundly, it is creating new ways to travel such as the massively game-changing Airbnb.

5. **They may not buy like Finders but they do think like them.** Evolving Finders are less responsive to big brands, mass marketing, and traditional authority.

6. **They skew younger but are not all young.** The two conditions of being young and being short of funds tend to go hand in hand yet there are Evolving Finders in every age bracket. Evolving Finders might not be in the position to choose a boutique resort holiday but will always behave with a quality-first ethic on more affordable levels. Like all Finders, Evolving Finders are the quality over quantity buyers in almost every lower cost purchase.

7. **Take an Evolving Finder over a Keeper any day.** While this is not the rich market of Finders, Evolving Finders provide more loyalty, profit, and safety from commoditization and downward price pressure than Keepers. And, they're only growing in power

8. **They are the new economic innovators.** The rise of "Hipster industry" indicates a set of career choices

among Evolving Finders that align with building real objects, a rejection of the career aspirations of the last few generations, and mobility between low and high tech careers.

15

◆

THE REVOLUTION WILL NOT BE ADVERTISED

The Millennial, Evolving Finder Manufacturer Economy

There are millions of Jasons all over the world today. Jason represents one of the most interesting emerging types of workers, careerists, voters, and consumers that have come along in quite some time. He might get a job, but then again he might go into some kind of business himself. If he does, Jason will belong to a sub-set of Evolving Finders, the Evolver Entrepreneur.

Evolving Finders are as individualistic as Finders – maybe more so. What makes them fascinating is that for the younger members of their sub-set, their place in life means fewer attachments than the more established Finder. It might be a case of chicken and egg but a sense of self-determination mixes well with the slim employment opportunities that exist in a post recessionary economy. It is in this world where, in spite of a strong level of education, large numbers of young Evolving Finders find themselves barred from the middle management ranks of a hollowing out middle class America.

Rugged Material is based in Cedar City, Utah. It has a passion for this one thing: products that last a lifetime.

Inspired by the craftsmanship of his father's still very much in use hundred-year-old saddle, company founder, Tyler Condie, decided to go into the "last a lifetime" business. It all began at Southern Utah University when, as an engineering student, Condie took on a design assignment as a challenge to create something that could simply not be worn out. He started out with a long series of prototype leather knife scabbards before arriving at that perfect, last a lifetime design. Soon the scabbards turned into bags and before long the designs turned into a business idea. To get things going and to raise money for a proper production facility, Condie launched a crowdfunding campaign through Kickstarter. It worked. His $15,000 appeal caught on and turned into more than $80,000. Today, Rugged Material, still based in Cedar City, sells hundreds of practically bombproof leather laptop cases, knife scabbards, bags, and more. Don't go looking for Rugged Material down at your local mall. One hundred percent of what they make can only be bought directly from the company through its online store.

John Randall's business card is made out of wood. Under his name is the address of his woodworking studio, Bien Hecho. It's located in Brooklyn's Old Navy Yards. Bien Hecho, which means "well made" in Spanish, specializes in custom furniture for homes. It is the wood, the source material, that really stands out on Bien Hecho's tables, bookcases, chairs, stools, and even beautifully crafted sawhorses; sawhorses that are more suited to supporting a stone or glass table top rather than a piece of gypsum board under a drywall knife. All of the wood is recovered and recycled. It is in this way that the furniture tells a story in two parts. First, with ultra-cool design and second, with a back story that is told by repurposed timbers and burls that have lived past lives in factory sheds, barns, buildings, and pilings.

The company's dedication to its craft takes on an extra dimension through education. Its woodworking class program teaches the near lost art of woodworking and cabinet making to customers and non-customers alike who belong to a generation that never knew a day when their furniture wasn't built in a factory in Poland, Mexico, or Vietnam.

There are thousands of Evolving Finder Entrepreneurs. They are opening up the roast and press-to-order coffee bar in an emerging neighborhood. They are cutting and sewing in a reinvigorated workshop space that makes bespoke jeans. They are the new craftspeople and artisans and brewmasters. They are resourceful people who are attracted to a do-it-yourself entrepreneurial ethos. There is no business without a buyer, but these Evolving Finder entrepreneurs and artisans have an excellent market for their wares in the form of the people who they actually understand as well as they understand themselves: Finders.

That is not to say that starting any kind of business is easy. It never has been and that isn't different today. However, funding is different, distribution is different, and promotion is different. And everything that is different about it sits in the comfort zone of Finders. Even more so among these millennial Evolving Finders.

Doing Business the Evolving Finder Way

In the world of the Evolving Finder Entrepreneur, there are products that range from the slightly mainstream to the slightly insane. In every case there are three ways that they differ from most conventional businesses: Funding, Distribution, and Promotion.

Crowdfunding: When the Banks Say No, the Crowd Says Show Us

Imagine yourself for a moment as a twenty-something commercial design graduate with no job, no credit rating, and no assets. You have an idea for a line of architectural blocks depicting cartoon versions of famous settings from legendary movies. These blocks can be purchased on your soon-to-be-live website. Before you get started you will need to rent shop space, buy and lease tools, have your website built, and hire a few people.

There are many banks in America today. There are banks all over the world. Now, go find one that will give you the $20,000 you need to get started. You might want to change out of that "vintage" Cookie Monster T-shirt before you get started but that's just a suggestion. Good luck.

In early April of 2009, the idea of getting a large and diverse set of strangers to fund a business enterprise was an unlikely and mysterious idea. By the end of that month there was Kickstarter – a crowdfunding framework based on the ages-old and mostly forgotten model of arts patronage where artists would ask their audiences and often-wealthy patrons to fund their work. Kickstarter offers patronage with a big difference. It is an entirely web-based model where users can behave as patrons and help to fund projects that they believe in. This they do in exchange for tangible and even intangible returns from those that they fund.

As of this writing, Kickstarter pledges have raised over $1.5 billion from 7.4 million donors (or backers) to help fund over 77,000 projects in over 90% of the world's countries. The range of funding is vast and diverse but always connects back to the funding model's mission to help bring creative projects to life. In this way, Kickstarter has helped to fund films, music, journalism, design, food and culinary-related endeavors, and, yes, Tyler Condie's Rugged Material bags.

Kickstarter's alignment with the arts, creativity, and even food makes it an area of interest for any Finder and his money out looking for a good time. Given what we have learned so far, one might never see a Keeper go online to fund sea-monster-inspired dinner plates called Calamityware, but there is a Finder or two, or 100, out there who would be all over it.

This brings us even closer to the special business relationship between Finders and Evolving Finders. Finders are more than just the customers for the entrepreneurial creative, through crowdfunding they are financing.

Given its association with the arts, music, film, and all the press that goes with those particularly attention-hogging industries, Kickstarter is perhaps the best-known crowdfunding organization out there. But it is far from alone.

Almost anything can find funding through this form. There is, for example, Indiegogo for business startups. There are crowd funds for charities like Crowdrise and FirstGiving. Does your dog need surgery? Then try personal crowdfunding with GoFundMe. The list grows every day. Not to say that everything gets funding. Crowdfunding is the ultimate meritocracy where great ideas and originality can often find their patrons.

The Great Shopping Mall in the Sky

In 2012, North American consumers spent $379 billion online. In 2014, the number was over $482 billion. Worldwide, ecommerce has eclipsed the $1.5 trillion mark with exponential growth accelerating with the adoption of technology in emerging economies. China has recently passed the United States as the world's largest ecommerce consumer and India is hot on its heels.

Finders were there first. Their trust and acceptance of technology and their love of the story behind the product make them the perfect online customer. Because of this, small start-up companies that specialize in anything from artisanal sausage to hand-tooled bicycle seats can go to market without ever needing to deal with a retail buyer, a manufacturer's representative, or a distribution company. For the small and specialized business, the route to the customer no longer needs to go down Main Street or negotiate the parking lot and the food court; it simply travels a straight line from maker to customer.

Internet purchases transcend bricks and mortar shopping on an even deeper level. Let us go back to Tina and her quest for the perfect egg. Her ideal might have been to talk to the actual egg farmer in person. Her natural tendency is to enjoy the realness of any purchase. This is where ecommerce works so well as a link between maker and buyer. Poppy Von Frohlich is a San Francisco based clothing designer and manufacturer. Their unique, pretty, and very cool coats, clothing, and accessories are made right there in San Francisco. You can go online right now, get yourself sized and order one or more of the artfully photographed pieces that are displayed on the site. You can't buy any of these pieces in a store but you can communicate directly with Trudy, the head of the company. If you would prefer, you can place a custom order made just for you. Something interesting is happening here – something that seems to speak of a bygone era. It has, somewhat ironically, been made possible by a new era of shopping. Today there is a kind of direct contact that hasn't really existed since the tailors and seamstresses disappeared from our main streets to be replaced by everything from Old Navy to Saks. Once again there is a direct dialogue between the proprietor of a manufacturing company and his or her customer. All of this made possible not by some post-apocalyptic return to horses and buggies and general goods stores but by an interactive portal into small artisan, craft-made, and design-based businesses. Brought to you by the Internet and expedited by the likes of PayPal and Federal Express.

The Best Kinds of Secrets Are Worth Repeating

Mass production, worker productivity, the loss of American jobs to China and beyond are for another book. An excellent read on those subjects can be found in Enrico Moretti's 2013 book, *The New Geography of Jobs*. One thing Moretti's book makes clear is that mass-produced goods are not going to stage a major comeback in North America. You will not see assembly lines filled with well-paid workers who whistle a happy tune while crafting fine bags, wallets, and iPad covers from recycled saddle leather. Far from it. In broad terms, most of what is mass-produced, as discussed in earlier chapters, is generally a commodity. These are goods that can be better and more cheaply manufactured overseas or, in the case of most domestic car production that employs heavy utilization of robots, without the touch of human hands.

The potential of the Evolving Finder-powered small business is in its ability to thrive in the niche of "non-mass produced" goods. These artisans, brewers, designers, and their like find a willing, premium-paying customer through their very individuality. The small scale of these businesses means another departure from the word "mass" in the irrelevance of mass marketing and its main driver, mass advertising.

The question then presents itself, "How do these companies ever get any business if no one knows they exist?" The answers are varied but the very rarity and individualistic essence of these products give them something that transcends the need for advertising. Instead these are products that contain something special that is shared between peers. The circle of direct influence between peers has always been a powerful force. Any restaurateur will tell you that success or failure depends on a collective set of positive or negative customer experiences. In the restaurant trade it is said that one rude server, one warm flat beer, or one fly in the soup can generate twelve negative word-of-mouth reviews, while one positive experience is lucky to generate two or three. It is human nature to quietly share the positive and loudly warn (complain) against the negative. Both positive and negative are now massively intensified by social media; word-of-mouth exchange is starting to be called social currency. But it's been around since men started wearing powdered wigs because that was what all the cool kids were doing.

That old chestnut, "Build a better mousetrap and the world will beat a path to your door," has its contemporary offspring. It is, "Build a better story and a world of people will find you on the Internet and talk about you on social media."

A Good Bag Makes its Own Friends

In 1993, a pair of Swiss brothers living in Zurich had a need for a good durable messenger bag. Markus and Daniel Freitag, both graphic designers, needed something that would keep their designs safe and dry while tooling around Zurich on that city's preferred form of transportation, the bicycle. Travel on any highway in Europe and you will see that almost all heavy transport trucks – Euro eighteen-wheelers if you will – use a trailer that is the same size as what you'll see in the slow lanes on the interstate. There is one difference. Instead of aluminum or fiberglass paneled sides, European semi-trailers cover their sides in heavy-duty rubberized cloth tarpaulins. These flexible, soft, but incredibly tough rubberized road warriors gave the brothers Freitag a very big idea. Once these truck tarps had lived out their useful lives on the road, the colorfully printed and diversely designed sheets of indestructability would wind up in landfills. Why not recycle them? Better yet, why not turn them into courier style commuter bags or what Markus and Daniel call "velo bags." With this, Freitag bags were born.

Each Freitag bag is made from a different section of any given truck tarp. This of course means that no two bags are exactly the same. The brothers don't call their enterprise a bag business. Instead Freitag is in the business of "R.I.P.s" which stands for "recycled individual products." Bags sell from just under $200 to $400 each. You can buy yours at one of about a dozen Freitag stores that have been constructed around Europe – also using recycled materials. In Zurich, for example, there is a store built out of nothing but used shipping containers. You can find one of their pop-up stores in Shanghai or Tokyo, go to one of their authorized dealers in Boston or San Francisco, or hunt down your own favorite R.I.P. on the busy online store that is also based in Zurich. When you do, your R.I.P will come in a minimalist reusable box. On the outside of that box you will find a digital photograph of the item it holds. Open the box, look inside and you'll find a handwritten note from one of the now 160 people who make the bags. It will say something like: "I'm Robert and I made this bag for you. Yes, I love you too."

Freitag has sold over 300,000 of these R.I.P.s and now makes everything from $60 iPhone sleeves to sets of luggage. In 2003, New York's Museum of Modern Art placed a Freitag brothers' bag in its designers' collection. It is in good company alongside the original iPod, Frank Lloyd Wright's side chairs, and the Slinkee.

Do an Internet search on Freitag and you will find a long list of articles on the company. One from Bloomberg speculates on the idea of the company going public (it won't). Go on Facebook and see their not-too-shabby 91,000 likes. Or have an experience similar to one that took place a few years back at an advertising awards show in Toronto where one Freitag owner, bag on shoulder, bumped into another Freitag owner who was carrying a purse made from what appeared to be part of the same tarpaulin. He made a new friend. The moral of this good product story isn't written by mass advertising, it is written by the product itself and broadcast by those who love it.

16

◆

WORLDS APART ON THE SAME PLANET

Beer sales are dropping while beer sales are growing. Electric cars are a bust and welcome to the electric car boom.

We are living in a world of contradictions. The volume and severity of those contradictions are at their best and their worst when things go terribly wrong in the economy. It is useful to look at the Great Recession of 2008, which, some would effectively argue, is still alive in 2015, for a closer examination.

How was Apple able to sell millions of iPhones, the most innovative (and pricey) mobile device the world had ever seen, right through its launch in the unhappy days of 2007 and into the financially apocalyptic months of 2008 and 2009? How did Apple then launch the iPad as a resounding success while most of the world economy was still going down in flames in 2010? The iPad? A product and a category that no one had ever heard of or knew they wanted? But there it was, selling like good luck charms at a giant game of Russian roulette.

Then came the Apple Stores, those beautifully designed, architecturally perfect, stand-alone retail victory laps that have proliferated in the world's great cities. Between those and their slightly smaller, mall-dwelling brethren they have created lineups of almost cultish customers in every corner of the Western, Eastern, and inevitably, emerging world. Yet, here is the contradiction: Circuit City, another retailer of things with screens and buttons – in fact far more of a selection of things with screens and buttons and speakers and headphones and ear buds and remote controls at far lower prices than a variety of similar appliances elsewhere – went spectacularly broke leaving 18 million square feet of empty store space and 34,000 employees out of work across America. How did this happen? On the face of it, it simply doesn't make any sense. Either the world has gone crazy or Circuit City inhabited an alternate universe. Bet on the latter.

Then, while Apple was doing its happy dance all over everyone else's sales per square foot statistics, the rest of America was watching a meltdown in Detroit that almost ended the life of the mighty General Motors and dropped the curtain on Pontiac, Saturn, and Saab and triggered the sell-off of Hummer, that proud symbol of Swartzeneggerism, to the Chinese.

Meanwhile, a little Japanese car company called Subaru moved into the fast lane of sales growth while everyone else drove over a cliff. Was Subaru's success some weird coincidence? Is it possible that some companies were able to develop immunity to economic downturns? Neither. Instead it was the way that Subaru's customers responded to the recession.

Hint: Subaru's customers were Finders.

Who's Afraid of the Big Bad Recession?

It is said that true character comes to the surface in times of crisis. For better or worse. The collective crisis that was the recent great recession helped to prove such a saying in the collective sense. It most certainly separated the Finders from the Keepers.

What happened? To begin with, Keepers did what Keepers do. Only more of it.

Bring up the subject of failures between 2008 and 2010 and almost any economist will point to a tightening of credit and an unemployment rate that rose by 5.3 percent over a two-year span. Unemployment in America sat at 4.7 percent in the pre-recession month of October 2007 and then hit 10 percent at rock bottom in October 2009. But even those figures do not fully explain a drop in some sectors of retail where the decline in sales far exceeded the actual impact of the recession.

A predictable thing happened in that fall of 2008 as markets crashed and the banks and then automakers went to the Federal Government for bailouts. When that happened, a large portion of the population, quite understandably, closed their wallets. Some, on the other hand, did not. And they weren't the so-called one percent.

Low Discretionary Spenders and Reverse Discretionary Spending Stimulation

During insecure times, Keepers experience what could be called the ultimate example of "reverse discretionary spending stimulation."

Keepers, those low spenders who need a high level of stimulation to part with their money in the first place, are highly receptive to powerful arguments against going shopping. Insofar as arguments against go, the recession was a whopper and it was both reasonably and hysterically reported by another powerful force of truth and authority in Keeper lives: mass and mainstream media. The result was that Keepers, very firmly and absolutely, stopped spending. Stimulation, in reverse, had been applied with a jackhammer.

The Great Price Dive

Imagine that things are just fine in the macro and microeconomics of the Keeper's world. A given retailer, say a home electronics retailer, publishes an advertising flyer. It is filled with low prices and special limited time offers, all of which are hot and tempting. It doesn't work.

A few days later that same store sends out another circular. It is absolutely splattered with 50% OFF offers and big DO NOT PAY FOR 180 DAYS financing deals and FREE BLENDERS FOR THE FIRST 50 CUSTOMERS. The results are about the same as the first try.

Knowing what we do about Keepers, these retail promotions feel like just the sort of thing that would get them moving during non-recessionary economic times. That is, unless there is another element in play. Try on this scenario. Say that our Keeper customers had inside knowledge that this particular store is prepared to take prices lower and lower. The retailer would keep doing so as long as the previous offer didn't work. Once customers showed up, the deals would find their equilibrium and the discounts would stop. Aha! But knowing this, customers could just stay home and watch the prices fall.

A waiting game would develop that would ultimately drive that retailer to a point where customers would almost need to be paid to take away merchandise.

This was exactly the effect that a heavily reported recession had on businesses all over the world. Its effects hit everything from bookstores to housewares stores to real estate developments. Consumers, most often those of the Keeper variety, not only stopped shopping but they stood by and waited to see how low things would go before finally buying. By the time anyone showed up at the checkout counter, the term profit margin had disappeared from the vocabulary of countless retail stores and businesses. In many cases, so had the term "open for business".

Homeowners found themselves underwater with their mortgages, or without a home. Credit went away. Unemployment went up by almost 6 percent. There were, of course, realities that came with the recession that wreaked havoc on the average consumer and prevented many from spending. Meanwhile the thrifty and cautious spirit of the Keeper served to amplify the negative effects of the recession.

Here's another thought. Why couldn't all of those retailers, manufacturers, and businesses who were out there getting their butts handed to them just switch customers and sell to all of those free spending Finders? Unfortunately it was too late for that. Finder brands kept their Finder customers and Keeper brands lost theirs. Yet the recession wasn't a total disaster in Keeperville. Businesses that were able to offer the pure unadulterated deal to Keepers did very well. Those who tried to walk the line between being something special to Finders while at the same time attempting to offer the GREATEST DEAL EVER to Keepers suffered. They suffered then and suffer now and will always be vulnerable to failure.

There is no middle ground. Not one that is sustainable. Not one that isn't terribly vulnerable. You just can't tell a Finder that your product is something to discover, that it is something of the finest quality, and completely unique while in the same breath say, "Oh, by the way, it is the cheapest thing on the market." You will lose your argument and his or her attention. Conversely, you can't tell a Keeper that your product is the cheapest while polluting your value message with pitches of quality, discovery, and uniqueness for a Finder. If you do, you are making it sound expensive to a Keeper, and cheap and second rate to a Finder.

A caution here, don't mistake the word "tell" as a proxy for advertising and marketing messages. Whatever you do, be it the quality of your product, where you sell it, what it looks, feels, sounds, and smells like is always telling a customer something.

Who won with the Keepers? The biggest boat. In March of 2009, Forbes Magazine reported that Walmart, the world's largest retailer, was one of the only stores to not only fend off declines but actually grow while deep in the heart of the U.S. recession. In the month of the Forbes report, year-on-year sales at the Walton family owned chain rose by 5.1%. Share dividends rose by 14.7%.

How could this happen? How could a store that sells almost anything and everything, one with a customer that is hanging around looking for the lowest prices, stay in business, let alone thrive? It all goes back to the art of fishing on the Sea of Keeper. As times get tight, only the biggest boat brings in the catch.

Contrast that with the second biggest boat in discount retail, Target, and you will see the difference. In the May 2009 article, Forbes reported that Target, with its position in the market as cheap chic, saw sales fall by 4.1%. It is worth noting here that a slight discretionary income bounce took place during that 2009 timeframe when gas prices fell, leaving a little more money in the pockets of the average consumer. Did this mean more shopping at more stores? No. It meant more shopping at one store: Walmart.

As prices fall, Keepers will wait for bottom. With its firm position as the biggest discounter, Walmart's brand conveyed the only thing that these reluctant shoppers really wanted to know: "Walmart means we have the lowest prices."

In *The Brand Gap*, Marty Neumeier's 2005 book on branding and design, the author talks about how a truly successful brand should equal just one word. Take a brand name and put an equal sign beside it. If you can, put one word on the other side of that equal sign as the one truthful description that lives in the minds of your consumer. If you can do this, (and most can't) you have an excellent brand. Among his examples was this one: Volvo = Safety.

Walmart, you can call it the biggest boat, you can call it your favorite store, or you can call it the evil empire. When it comes to the essence of Walmart's success during and after a recession, you can use Neumeier's exercise to calculate this potent and unassailable equation: Walmart = Cheapest.

Other retailers could print edition after edition of increasingly desperate flyers – they did and it didn't work. They could produce ever more shrill television and radio ads. They could drop their prices, they could offer to mow their customer's lawns with lawnmowers sold at 90% off retail, and accept the grass clippings as coupons. It just didn't matter because in the minds of their intended customers, someone else was already there at the bottom of all pricing. It was Walmart and no matter how low the prices would go, the biggest boat was built to navigate them. Profitably.

Look around today and of course you will see that our friends at Target, those captains of the second biggest boat, didn't sink during the great recession; they just took on water. Target's brand position next to Walmart is, as mentioned above, cheap chic. It relies more on discretionary purchases from its customers. About three-fifths of its sales fall into that category. We don't live in a consuming world where large segments of the population make do with one pair of shoes; so, yes, Keepers do make discretionary purchases. They just do so far less frequently than Finders. When they do, Keepers are still primarily stimulated by the deal. That is where Target fits into the Keeper world. But when the discretionary wallets slam shut, the smart money is on Walmart. That is where Target took on water; the retailer had its deepest drop, 6.2% in year-on-year, same-store sales, between August 31, 2008 and August 31, 2009. Although the red roundel fell far behind its rival, it was still in one piece once the recovery took hold in 2011. Target was saved by the migration of wealthier shoppers who moved down-market from department stores. No, they weren't Finders. For the most part, they were wealthy Keepers.

Yet Walmart even wins with Finders. Finders are always far more likely to be in discretionary spending mode but look on non-discretionary purchases as commodities. They will, without the coupon-clipping fervor of the most ardent Keeper, pay the bottom dollar. A Finder will be looking for the lowest price on a commodity purchase – they just won't work as hard at it. This gives Walmart another advantage. To a Finder, Walmart as "Walmart = Cheapest" is the ultimate brand-as-mental-shortcut to buying what they don't care about at the lowest possible price. With the Walmart brand, Finders have a place to buy what they're indifferent to and don't have to think about it either.

Finders do have a favorite in their non-discretionary purchases, one that provides a certain level of exclusivity through its membership-only selling, has a jaw dropping return policy, and often has more interesting and sometimes even definite products and that is Costco.

The Wealthy Keeper Waiting Game

To a Wealthy Keeper, downward price pressure is a wonderful thing. Imagine a world where prices just keep going down. Even better, imagine a world where you have plenty of money on hand. This sounds good, particularly if you happen to be a person who enjoys gathering a volume of goods such as conspicuously expensive brands of watches, fast boats, and luxury penthouse condominiums. Wealthy Keepers, those deal-driven conspicuous consumers, can treat a recession like a trip to hog heaven. When a recession signals the opportunity to buy goods that were once worth more, it furnishes a bargaining position that not only lets that buyer get that high-status item for far less, but it also comes with the bragging rights to the deal he or she cut getting it. When a high-flying Keeper walks into a recession-made bargain basement, he can dance in delight to what he considers to be one of the most beautiful phrases on earth, "cents on the dollar."

17

◆

CRISIS? WHAT CRISIS?

Every economic era brings fresh words and phrases into the common lexicon. In the years that surrounded the crash of 2008, perhaps the most attractive ones – spoken by politicians, investors, and business folk with a faraway look and a wistful lilt were, Recession Proof.

When the great recession struck, the world came to an end. And, it didn't.

While property developments, large retailers, carmakers, and corner delis died gory deaths, some companies just grew and grew. There was a common thread that ran between these trend-bucking companies. It was their customer, the Finder.

No one wakes up one morning and says, "I think I'll get some customers of a very particular type. By golly they will make me profitable. They will help me to be a better employer. They will support me in my quest to provide superior products, services, and experiences." No one ever woke up the next morning and said, "While I'm at it, I'll make myself recession-proof by targeting customers who aren't afraid of recessions." Finder businesses were never developed to go after a Finder or whatever one might have been calling them. In fact, there never really was a business that started out as a Finder's business. Businesses got that way because Finders found them. And more often than not, Finders created them.

Yes, a recession is a great way of turning up the volume on failure but even more so it is a very instructive way of unearthing the reasons for success.

18

◆

THE LITTLE CAR THAT COULD KICK YOUR ASS

Subaru

Bruce and Sue live outside Marin City, just north of San Francisco. The two have been married since their days at Berkley. That was in the late 1960s. No, they are not and never have been hippies. Bruce is an engineer who has spent his career in the oil and gas industry. Sue is an occupational therapist freshly retired. The two used to be something of a rarity. They might be called the original Finders. By looking at them you'd have a hard time telling that Bruce and Sue are now in their early seventies. A passion for windsurfing on Sue's part and a healthy addiction to mountain biking on Bruce's might have kept them so well preserved. Or it could be the organic vegetables that come out of their backyard garden. Or both. At any rate, these two are still quite capable of hitting the trails of Marin and the windsurfer's paradise located outside their weekend home in nearby Bolinas. Bruce's job has taken the couple and their now grown children all over the world with stops in Australia, Asia, and the Middle East. Today Bruce and Sue's driveway, high in the Marin hills, contains two cars. They are both Subarus. One is currently in use and the other, like Bruce, is semi-retired. Again like Bruce, it has a lot of miles on it, well over 400,000. That particular car is Subaru number five in a total of six Subarus that the couple has owned. It seems that Bruce and Sue think that they might be on to a good thing.

When the recession bit hard in 2009, every automaker doing business in the United States took a shellacking. Except Subaru. This subsidiary of Japan's Fuji Heavy Industries and maker of boxer-engined, all-wheel-drive cars bucked the crash in a big way. While others sold far fewer cars in 2009 than in the same period of 2008, Subaru enjoyed a 15% jump in sales. This was in the face of an industry average decline of 21%! Those are not numbers that are biased by disproportionate declines among particular automakers. They do not even speak of countries of origin. Among Japanese automakers during these dark days and sleepless nights, Toyota sales dropped 19%, Honda lost 19%, and Nissan dropped 18%.

To some, a car is like a set of clothes that you drive around in, a reflection of character and personality. To others it is nothing but pure utility. In total is everything you see on the road. If money doesn't factor into it and you want a beautiful car, you might start with Ferrari and work your way down through the price ranges, perhaps stopping at Jaguar, then maybe Audi, and then even Mazda. In every case there are different levels of interesting and appealing curved lines and evocations, real or imagined, of sleekness and high performance that run from supercar to student car. One could argue that a BMW or a

✗ 4 CYLINDER HORIZONTALLY OPPOSED

Nissan would be the better aesthetic choice but beauty is always a subjective debate. If one were to look at reliability, a similar journey might take place through many cars but would probably land on Toyota with stops along the way at Honda and perhaps, less convincingly, Mercedes Benz. Reliability is a more objective argument that can easily be backed up with reams of data and consumer reports.

Let's talk about an off-road car. There is only one brand of car that is and always has been that one thing, off-road. Subaru has been building on its original concept of a boxer-engine, all-wheel-drive car since it appeared in America in 1968. Subjective debates aside, a Subaru would seldom win any arguments on the beauty measure. It would win on reliability. Dig around a little and you will find that Subaru is consistently rated at the top of predicted and experienced reliability ratings from almost every consumer testing body in existence.

In consumer shorthand, Subaru can be boiled down to just one true thing, the off-road car. Other cars are many things; Audi, another recession-bucking car and Finder favorite, is the leader in luxury all-wheel-drive vehicles; Toyota, as the world's biggest carmaker, makes many different cars, trucks, minivans, sporty cars, and SUVs. With a few somewhat tragic exceptions, Toyota still holds bragging rights to a high-quality product with the reliability ratings that come with that well-founded claim. Subaru, on the other hand, just makes the off-road car.

It would be easy for Subaru to build its brand around product attributes that can be associated with its status as the definitive off-road car. In this way, the company could "brand position" itself with easily substantiated claims of durability that could be expressed in a more general sense and then pitch itself to a wider audience. That would be a typical broad-appeal compromise and, as it is with so many other companies, automotive and otherwise, they would create a brand that doesn't really stand for anything at all. No, in Subaru's case, the conditions of durability and reliability are just the simple result of what the car is made for. They are the minimum requirement for a vehicle that is expected to consistently manage a bunch of muddy back-roads on the way to any number of ski, kayak, mountain bike, camping or other suitably out-of-the-way destinations.

Now let us <u>not</u> imagine this scene as a cut from <u>every SUV commercial ever made</u> – the one that usually features a cute, three-year-old girl who sits comfortably and securely in an unrealistically child-goo-free booster seat. In said commercial, our super cute kid will smile approvingly and adorably as Daddy and his brave and agile "your-brand-here SUV" avoid a collapsing mountainside. These unoriginal and ubiquitous SUV commercials are no more than a focus-group polished attempt to qualify any brand of carmaker for a run at a perceived brand position – a brand position that says the brand is "off-road-ish." Staged proof is just that, staged. Subaru is real proof. Real proof is forty-six years of building pretty much the same car. One that isn't just designed to go off-road but built for, tested for, and dedicated to real off-road capability. It is done at the opportunity cost of getting into, for example, the minivan business. A Subaru is living proof of its performance. Not while imitating a Jeep or a Land Rover. Just by being a Subaru.

Those of you who know a little about the Subaru product line might say, "The Forester is an SUV." Not really. Built from the ground up like a Subaru, it's more of a tall car. A tall off-road car.

Also, like most SUVs and all-wheel-drive cars, a Subaru will spend the vast majority of its life on-road. So why the focus on off-road? Interestingly, that's not really the point. Returning to our generic SUV commercial for a moment, we can see that almost every car manufacturer wants to market at least part of its product line as some brawny, durable entity. Those features might actually be put to use from time to time. If they are not, they may at least help the owner to be seen as rugged and adventurous. This is precisely the phenomenon that has been filling parking lots (and gas stations) with quite unnecessary SUVs for decades.

The difference is the customer. Subaru owners approach outdoor adventures from the standpoint that isn't an ideal – it is a reality. They are not thinking, "If I buy this car I will look like I'm outdoorsy and adventurous," or even, "If I buy this car I will become outdoorsy and adventurous." Subaru buyers are already there. They are thinking more along the lines of, "I can get my kayak to the river without getting stuck." Subaru owners aren't into an idealized sense of the outdoors; they see the outdoors as a part of their very existence. In this way they look at the car in a far more pragmatic way, one that can't really be communicated through advertising or "brand positioning." It just has to be real. And forty-six years of the same engine and proven all-wheel-drive system gets you exactly that. Real.

You might be asking then, "Why haven't they been making SUVs?" Okay, you could argue that they have, but we can return to practical elements that separate those who buy an idea, or a brand, from those who buy a pure product. First, any true mountain biker, road biker, kayaker, surfer, canoeist, windsurfer, skier, or snowboarder will tell you that it is one heck of a lot easier to deal with the roof rack that sits on a car rather than on a SUV. Sure an SUV is okay for the occasional weekend warrior but to anyone who loads and unloads a couple of 12-foot paddleboards from a roof rack more than once a week, an SUV is literally a pain in the back.

Secondly, if an individual is buying a vehicle for its realness of utility, then the question, "Why an off-road car when most of its life is spent on road?" is automatically answered. Real utility does not call for a big and tall vehicle for everyday driving. The purpose-built, off-road car is far more functional through every part of its existence than that "maybe-sometimes" off-road-ish behemoth.

Subaru does advertise, a little, and even though the company's marketing budget is comparatively miniscule, this is where the brand separates itself once again.

Before we get into that, let us take a short trip away from cars and talk about something almost as sexy: a really good blender.

Prove It or Lose It

In 1999, Tom Dickson realized that he could build a better blender. Using a more powerful motor, a different shaped jug, and a carefully redesigned blade made of extremely strong steel he did just that. Blendtec was born. The product was strong, durable, capable of blending pretty much anything, and built to last a lifetime. Dickson had built the better blender. But, in reality and in a world of Osters, Cuisinarts, Black & Deckers, and Kenmores, Blendtec was a brand that would just barely survive on the fringes of obscurity. That changed in 2006 when newly minted Marketing Director, George Wright, noticed a pile of sawdust on the company's factory floor. He enquired as to its origins and was informed that the pureed pulp had once been a sturdy 2 x 4 piece of wood. Running a 2 x 4 through a blender was just another standard "can we break it?" test that the Blentec staff had come up with. Evidently the Blendtec blenders were pretty hard to break. That gave Wright an idea. Armed with a cheap video camera, a set of ear protectors, and a lab-coat-wearing demonstrator in the form of Blendtec founder Tom Dickson himself, the "Will it Blend?" YouTube series was born. I recommend you stop reading right now, do a "Will It Blend" YouTube search, and then watch in awe as Tom stuffs everything from a box of golf balls to a full sized Apple iPad into a blender. You can even thrill as Justin Bieber's hardcover autobiography goes into the insatiable blender's gaping maw.

In every case, Dickson hits a switch and turns everything into various versions of powdered smithereens. It is jaw-dropping stuff.

There is all kinds of advertising in this world, but even the most hipster-bearded, espresso quaffing advertising creative director will have to admit that nothing beats a good product demonstration. As far as product demonstrations go, you would have a hard time beating a blender that turns a pile of hockey pucks into rubbery dust. Did it work? Let's begin with another fact. There was, and still is, no media budget at all for Blendtec. This means no TV, radio, or newspaper ads, and no billboards or skywriting. Correspondingly, it also means that instead of acting as docile target markets for paid advertising, potential customers actually sought out, found, and, most importantly, shared Blendtec's marketing efforts. Watch a bowl full of cell phones get turned into some sort of apocalyptic talc by the furiously spinning blades and you might do the same thing: share it with your friends. So what did this kind of radical demonstration do for the company? Sales of Blentec grew by 700%.

What else happened? Blendtec conclusively proved its way into the top of the brand pile. It transcended a very crowded and mature category and made the rest of the pack look like a bunch of second-rate blenders destined to fight it out in a price battle. In achieving all of that, Blendtec shows us one simple and crucial fact. In the face of true proof, claims are nothing.

Subaru proved it. They demonstrated and demonstrated and

demonstrated. When they did, you didn't see the same little girl from that generic SUV commercial. If you did, someone would surely get arrested for child endangerment. Subaru has been deeply involved with off-road rally racing since 1980 and has spent almost all of that time as a dominant force in this fast, filthy, and downright death-defying form of motorsport. Even today, the iconic blue and yellow of the cars that Subaru used during its long tenure in the World Rally Championships resonate in memory. Even though the company's time in that series ended in 2008, those colors still serve as something that approach a second logo. Those race rally cars are modified but only to a point; they use the same symmetrical four-wheel-drive system that is on every Subaru on the road and the same engine – the boxer engine. (In case you are wondering, a boxer engine arranges its piston banks across from each other so that, for example, a four cylinder engine uses two banks of two cylinders arranged a 180 degree angle firing in opposite directions; this is unlike the usual "straight" arrangement where all cylinders are arranged in the same row, or a V where two banks are arranged in a, you guessed it, V.) Almost every manufacturer on the planet has at least dipped its toe into motorsport but this is different. Subaru's place in rally racing can easily be contrasted against the presence of many car manufacturers in such categories as stock car racing where any resemblance between the racing car and its showroom counterpart is coincidental. On top of this, Subaru's rally racing commitment is contextual. No sane person who plans on living a long life and retaining a drivers license would engage in the kind of driving seen in almost all racing, but, in the case of Subaru, owners see versions of their actual cars demonstrating real-world off-road capabilities in the most extreme sense while rally racing. Unlike what happens on a conventional Nascar loop, NHRA drag strip, or Formula One circuit, rally races and endurance rallies take place on almost exactly the same kind of roads and surfaces that Subaru owners will actually drive on.

No one in their right mind would stick their iPad in a Blendtec either. But anyone that has seen any of the YouTube demonstrations will surely be convinced of this blender's durability. It stands to reason that a machine that can eat a 2 x 4 can be counted on to blend a Margarita. On the road, the same goes for Subaru.

As for those slightly wilder souls, the off-road automotive equivalents of those who would actually just love to blend up a hockey puck smoothie, Subaru offers the twin turbo, intercooled 268 horsepower WRX STI. Please blend safely.

Finders want the real authentic. Subaru has done everything that needed to be done to prove itself as the realest of the real as an off-road car. Yet, that would only matter if an off-road car were a relevant product for Finders. It is. Finders are risk takers. Finders play outside. They go and find, they explore. Subaru isn't just a vehicle that gets them there – it's the very best one for the job. Finders are four times more likely to ski, twice as likely to surf, and 50 percent more likely to jog. Finders are into human powered sports. Drive by the parking lot of any REI on a Saturday morning and you will see a piece of pavement decorated with four-wheeled evidence of the match in interests between Finders and Subaru.

What About Brand?

BMW is a good example of a big brand. It is a luxury brand and it is well established as a status symbol. There is another fact that tends to get forgotten under those signals of status and luxury: BMW makes great cars to drive. Many Finders who love to drive will consider the Bayerische Motoren Werke product to be the best driver's car on the road. So they will buy the product but, almost perversely, they will buy it in spite of the BMW brand (and everything else that goes with it). In the case of Subaru, that company's position on the fringes of mainstream makes it almost an anti-brand. Unlike BMW, Mercedes, Dodge RAM, or Ford, it isn't a brand that ever leans on its name to claim anything. It stands on its product. This makes Subaru a product that comes before its brand.

Finally, it's not even about the price. In a 2012 article titled, "Are Subarus the best cars money can buy?" *Fortune Magazine* reported that Subaru customers are generally quite capable of affording a more expensive vehicle. They added that the company's loyal customers continued shopping right through recessions with the words, "even when the economy takes a dive." The same year the article was published, sales of what *Fortune Magazine* calls the "artisanal car" were up 26%.

19

◆

THIS DUD'S FOR YOU

The Great Beer Contradiction

There are sixty-four microbreweries in San Diego. Beer sales are falling. Craft beers sales are growing by 13.9% per year.

How could all of these things be happening at the same time? In 2013, big beer brands in America dropped in sales by an average of 3.9%. Those figures could seem like a temporary aberration. They're not. Before calculating any gains in craft beer, it is useful to note that this entire beer category has been leaking all over the bar top. According to Gallup, beer drinking among eighteen to twenty-nine year olds fell from 71% during 1992 to 1994, to 41% during 2012 to 2013. Concurrent to the drop in beer consumption, another Gallup report showed that liquor consumption rose from 13% to 28%, and wine drinking rose from 14% to 24%. Data, research, and consumer trends can explain a lot of this. Tastes have changed. Hard liquor is in ascendancy. Wine is the thing now. What about a dietary trend? Beer isn't gluten free. In 2013, the NPD Group reported that 30% of U.S. adults said that they intended to reduce or eliminate their gluten intake. That could be a trend but even if it is, it's more bad news for the purveyors of the barley sandwich.

But then there's craft beer, swimming upstream against all that downstream current.

Back to the bad news. By looking at those facts and figures we can see a future where Bud isn't quite the King of Beers, maybe just the old rich uncle.

What happened to beer is analogous to what happened to many perennial brands that we have all grown up with. Their very ubiquity has caused them to wear on us like an overplayed pop song. Get in your car and drive by a gas station or a convenience store and you'll see what you've already seen at any point in time over the past decade. These are the indicators of big beer brand decline printed in DayGlo on roadside reader boards or slickly designed vinyl banners provided by the brands themselves. They all say the same thing, "Big Deals on Beer." In other words, cheap beer.

The big beer brands have spent the past ten, twenty, even thirty years employing a can't-miss strategy that works on two fronts. Part one – build a brand around what even the most ardent big brand beer-o-phile would call a pretty mediocre product. It goes something like this: build those brands and build them like crazy with everything from celebrity endorsements to monstrous sports and entertainment sponsorships to, of course, gargantuan advertising budgets. The objective of these campaigns? To be the brand at the top of Joe Sixpack's mind before those other big beer bastards get there – and do it by being everywhere that Joe is, might be, and isn't. It is easy to run out of adjectives when describing the size of big beer advertising expenditures. According to Dementer Group's 2013 report, America's two largest brewing companies, Anheuser-Busch InBev and MillerCoors, spent a combined $11 billion on advertising, marketing, and sales between 2009 and 2013 – $11,219,100,000 to be exact.

The next time you open an advertising circular or flyer for a local supermarket, look for the beer specials. Spot one and give it a read. More often than not, about half of the advertising cost of that "save on cheap beer" ad has been paid for, in cash or rebate, by the brewery. Welcome to part two of the can't-miss beer sales strategy, the "special retail offer." Sometimes that offer comes from a discount that the brand offers the retailer, sometimes it's the retailer who cuts a bit of margin. Often it is both. You won't have a hard time finding these deals. In fact, just try going shopping any time without seeing one of the big brewers on sale.

What we wind up with is something that is actually more about brand than actual product. Big beer seems to have little to do with anything but mass production and scale. Its sales message is always about immediacy and it drives that immediacy with price and price only.

Ladies and gentlemen, what we have here is the perfect Keeper product. But, as Keepers age, they drink less beer.

Ross Honeywill and Verity Blyth's 2006 book *NEO Power* reports that NEOs (Finders), are best represented in the twenty-five to thirty-nine year old age group. This is an age range when education levels and employment mean the financial ability to become a full-fledged Finder. Yet that more millennial half of the Finder Equation, the Evolving Finder, is well represented in the twenty-one to twenty-nine age bracket where the real beer drinkers can be found. It's not that those Evolving Finders aren't drinking beer – they're just not drinking big brand beer.

It's 4:30 on a Wednesday afternoon in Fairfax, is a hilly, tree-covered suburb parked in the middle of Marin County, California. The past ten years have been good to this region. The post Internet bubble growth of nearby Silicon Valley and the bounce back in venture capital and banking in San Francisco have created a solid economy filled with talented, well educated, and very well paid innovators. Property values are high and there are no "for lease" signs on the main and side streets of Fairfax.

Customers are starting to roll up to the outdoor picnic tables and indoor booths of the DIY looking interior at Iron Springs Pub and Brewery and Community. And they are, quite literally, rolling up from their afternoon mountain bike rides. Those with more conventional working hours will arrive later, in many cases after their Wednesday afternoon rides on the trail covered hills that surround the area.

When they get here they won't be ordering anything that they might have seen in a TV commercial or on the side of a blimp. They will be ordering a Casey Jones IPA or a wooden paddle covered in six tasters. The beer isn't brewed in Milwaukee or in the "Heart of the Rockies;" it's brewed about thirty feet from that picnic table out front. Sure, there will be a few that order a plate of nachos but it is just as likely that someone will be having Marin meatloaf made with organic grass-fed chuck. Maybe with a side of black lentils.

At $5.25 a pint, there are cheaper beers to be found in Marin – but not by much. Tonight there is a featured beer on offer. They are calling it Ale for ALS. When you order one, $2 goes to fund a local ALS charity. Ask the waitress Fiona, about her job at Iron Springs and she'll tell you that after her job at Applebee's, she had never wanted to waitress again. "I grew up in Michigan and never finished college. I had a job making minimum wage at Applebee's. I hated being a waitress. Then I moved out to Marin and got this job just to get started. I've been here three years and I love it. The people are great, we really care about what we serve, and we are always giving back to the community. I'm making $15 an hour, plus tips, and I have a great medical plan. I love my job."

Michael Altman is a brewmaster from Colorado. Eleven years ago he moved out here with his family. He came for the chance to do something that was his own and Iron Springs Pub, Brewery and Community was created from this vision. You'll note the word "community" in the name of the place. "I can brew my beer and really be a part of the community here," says

Altman. It goes without saying that there is a lot more going on at this brewpub than what you'll find in a case of cold ones at your local convenience store. Which brings up an interesting concept, one that transcends the simple notion that Finders like micro, craft, or brewpub beer. Finders help create better jobs. In the case of Iron Creek, Finders, simply by the act of drinking better beer, help to support a better community.

There are sixty-four brewpubs in San Diego. There are, as of today, fifty-eight in Portland, Oregon. According to Dementer Group, the big three – Coors, Miller, and Budweiser, and their sub brands and holdings, represent 75% of the U.S. beer market and have been losing share at a rate of about 3.9% over a two-year period while craft beer has grown by 13.9% over the same time. What is interesting to observe is that this report only covers packaged beers purchased at retail and doesn't take into account the proliferation of thriving brewpubs across America.

Which takes us back to our brewpub in Fairfax and across the street to The Good Earth Organic Market. Let us ignore the fresh organic produce, artisanal cheeses, and earth friendly cleaning products (and organic eggs) for the moment and head for the beer cooler. There you'll find cases, bottles, and growlers with names like Big Bad Baptist and Yeti Imperial Stout. These are just two names out of the thousands of independent craft brew brands that are creating the opportunity for beer drinkers to try something delicious with character at a price that doesn't really push anyone out of the affordability frame. The Demeter

Group's report goes on to categorize this burgeoning new beer customer as the "extremist." There is another name for those who like to explore their beer for themselves and evaluate it based on the beer itself as opposed to the brand or the price. These drinkers are not extremists. They are Finders and Evolving Finders.

20

◆

THE SWEET SMELL OF SALES PER SQUARE FOOT

Anthropologie

An old realtor's trick that advises that if you want to make a good impression on prospective buyers, bake some cookies. That piece of advice is even more relevant when the home in question contains a cocktail of scents that range from fresh baked lasagna to fresh filled diaper. Realtors know that scent is a powerful trigger. No retailer seems to understand this better than Anthropologie. Enter one of the 175-and-counting versions of this offshoot of Philadelphia-based Urban Outfitters and your olfactory system goes into sensory overdrive. Today it might be bergamot or it might be something that evokes rain falling on flowerbeds.

Walk into a pharmacy and it smells like medicine. Walk into a furniture store, it smells like polish, glue, and (hopefully) wood. Soap stores smell like soap stores. Enter the wall of scent that is any one of over 850 worldwide Lush Handmade Cosmetics stores. Take in the loaves, bars, balls, and blocks of soaps, cosmetics, and flower bath bombs and you might even be knocked backward a few steps by its sweet and busy barrage of perfumes and scents. But clothing stores, well, they usually smell like clothing stores. Perhaps the smell of clothing is literal but when you really inhale deeply, it generally smells a bit like a mixture of carpet and window cleaner. An Anthropologie smells like a lot of things but it doesn't smell like a clothing store. For the most part, it smells like a good mood.

Then there's the music – it might be a French torch singer, or it might be The Monkees. The days of Muzak are well behind us and contemporary music in any retail setting is commonplace. While you can probably get a hit of Black Sabbath at your local supermarket, you will certainly hear some Matchbox 20. It is highly unlikely that you will hear Shonen Knife or Phoenix. Anthropologie programs music that isn't based on the common idea of familiarity, instead it creates an aural environment that manages to be attractive by being, at best, only vaguely familiar. How unique is this? Anthropologie playlists are available online and listened to outside of the store, presumably by customers who are nowhere near an Anthropologie. In a case of retail as radio, one can go to music streaming services such as Spotify or Last FM and actually stream an Anthropologie playlist.

Some will tell you Anthropologie doesn't smell or sound like a clothing store because it isn't a clothing store. This would be true in part; every Anthropologie sells a variety of eclectic merchandise. You can buy doorknobs, dishes, and books there, which might feel a bit like something that might detract from the focus of the available clothing and fashions. Candles and incense can be found all over the store and certainly play a part in those scents that waft around the places. But Anthropologie is to a very large degree a clothing store and is most certainly a fashion store. It is a fashion store that manages to be a women's clothing store for Finders. Outfits run around the $250 mark and shoes around $400. By price alone, it defines itself as a premium store and indeed aims itself at women in households earning upward of $200,000 per year. At those prices and with that market, one might be tempted to call the place a bit exclusive and upscale. That would be inaccurate. Anthropologie avoids becoming exclusionary through its smaller pieces and by doing so offers itself up as a bohemian housewares store for Evolving Finders.

There is much to be seen and analyzed from the in-store experience. Everything that the retail product does can help to define Anthropologie as a Finder Brand, but perhaps what makes it so is best said in the company's own words:

"Anthropologie is a lifestyle brand that imparts a sense of beauty, optimism and discovery to our customer. For her, Anthropologie is an escape from the everyday; it is a source of inspiration and delight, where innovative merchandising, customer centricity and a curated array of products come together to create an unimagined experience."

Well put. Here is a company that has corporate values that reflect those of a Finder. But values are only useful when seen in action. In fact, corporate values that aren't put into action at the customer level go by another name, "happy horseshit." Finders, with their love of real authenticity, their search for the story, and their healthy lack of respect for authority, can smell happy horseshit from a mile away and will quickly run in an entirely different direction. By delivering on its stated values, and by doing so consistently and on an everyday basis, Anthropologie has staked its place in the Finders world.

Why is this extraordinary? Because it is such a rare thing to come across a corporate mission statement or statement of company values that is actually experienced at the customer level at all. In some cases the customer doesn't even come up in the mission statement. Think about this the next time you fly a major U.S. carrier. Here, for example, is American Airline's Mission Statement:

"AMR Corporation is committed to providing every citizen of the world with the highest quality air travel to the widest selection of destinations possible. AMR will continue to modernize its fleet while maintaining its position as the largest air carrier in the world, with the goal of becoming the most profitable airline. AMR is the airline that treats everyone with equal care and respect, which is reflected in the way each AMR employee is respected. AMR recognize that its employees are the key to the airline's success and invests in the futures in lives of its employees. By investing in tomorrow's technologies and by following a strict adherence towards environmental regulations, AMR demonstrates its commitment to the world environment."

There are worthy points here but what do they mean or, more importantly, what do they do for a customer? There's an obvious lack of mention for customers in this mission statement, and let us not forget that this is a business that is entirely funded by the customer. You could consider the term "citizen of the world" as a mention of that living, breathing, and ticket-buying organism stuffed into the middle seat in row thirty-two, but "citizen of the world" seems to be a customer description framed in the vaguest terms.

Disconnection between corporate values and customer experience is incredibly commonplace. Perhaps with some companies a customer might experience a nuance of what is printed on a framed poster that is hung in the reception area of a head office but those instances are, for the most part, rare. This brings us to a crucial point in the Anthropologie story – one that tends to repeat itself with any successful company and most certainly with any company or organization that has the foresight, imagination, or courage to appeal to and hold the Finder as a customer. Here it is.

Values at the top = Values at the bottom.

For the sake of convenience, we can call ownership and upper management the "top" and the customer the "bottom" but those two positions ought to be interchangeable. In this case it's good to look at the customer experience as something that sits on top, with the organization acting as the foundation of that experience at the bottom. In any case, values will translate all the way through the organization and land with the customer. When it works, it is often because those values are set by strong leadership, or just one extremely effective and visionary business leader and executed properly through that leadership. However, this is a process that is extremely fragile and often quite volatile. Values can be easily eroded. Their journey from an ideal at the boardroom level to true manifestation at the customer level, with all of its attendant touch points, can be an extremely rocky one. It is one thing to say, "We are in the business of surprising and delighting our customers." Those are powerful words when stated inside the comfortable confines of a mini-bar or equipped corner office. It is quite another thing to act on that kind of statement through every senior, middle, and junior executive, general manager, manager, supervisor, and employee in every nook and cranny of purchasing, finance, operations, logistics, marketing, customer service, real estate, interior design, and building maintenance, to name a few.

As a brief experiment, recite your company's mission statement. If you got it right you might just be on to something. If you got it wrong – and that means anything from an inaccurate recitation to a shrug along with the words, "I didn't know we had one," you can absolve yourself of guilt (at least for the time being) with the knowledge that at least 90 percent of respondents do just as poorly as you just did.

But, make no mistake, it's important. Great customer experiences that Finders seek, discover, buy, and become fiercely loyal to, come from companies who make sure that their values are out there for all to see.

Values at the top equals values at the bottom is a balance

that starts with what burns in the heart of whoever is leading a particular company. However, this can become a problem when a particular leader leaves, either by choice, after a hefty buy-out, or by force. In any case, this obvious problem can be seen time and again. It happens when a leader like Howard Schultz leaves Starbucks to be replaced by another more operations-focused leader (often a Keeper) who works in more pragmatic and money-saving ways. It happened when the late Steve Jobs left Apple the first time. (Nothing can be said of his second and tragically all-too-early second exit). It might be happening now at Lululemon without Chip Wilson to apply his yoga/hippie/big-mouthed navigation to that Finder-beloved company.

True corporate values at the customer level are not something you read in a hallway on the way to a restroom in a chain restaurant. To really get to the customer, those values must be alive and carry a whole set of really meaningful manifestations. For example, Anthropologie.

Let's take a core sample from that Anthropologie company mission statement. We'll apply it to scent and sound. Pull out just two words, "unimagined experience." With those two words available for examination we can think about music. A given customer may never before have heard a single note of what is playing inside an Anthropologie, but she will at the very least catch a bit of it and, on a barely conscious level, enjoy it for the first time. Then there is that scent that can't quite be placed but feels good. These are just sensory touch points that are experienced well before any good old-fashioned shopping has taken place. They are just a small part of the retailer's "unimagined experiences" – experiences that aren't seen – they are *felt*. The experiences are also not expected (imagined); they just show up. It's just a smell, but it's one of a big set of manifestations that transport Anthropologie's values from top to bottom. These "unimagined experiences" are felt before so much as a pair of "I-have-never-seen-these-before-I-must-have-them" boots are found, tried-on, tested on the board floors, and bought. They are felt before a Bauhaus-style drawer pull is dropped into an interesting looking shopping basket.

Let us take another corporate values core sample: "curated array of products." There are no two Anthropologie stores that are exactly alike. Anthropologie achieves this seemingly anti-retail chain act thought a number of strategies. One effective strategy is that Anthropologie does a portion of its buying from artisans, artists, and designers in the store's immediate area. The chain is careful not to stretch these small-scale suppliers beyond their capacities. It will not swamp them with anything that approaches a chain-wide order; instead the retailer will simply purchase an achievable order, sell part of it locally and then ship the rest to another market or two so that the artist will get exposure in a different geographical area. This of course serves the artist but let's remember that this is retail, not an art gallery that works on consignment. What serves the brand is the uniqueness of items sourced from the local artisans, which translates into a sense of discovery for the Anthropologie customer – and a healthy margin for Anthropologie.

The idea of creating no two stores alike is a diversion from retail's common buying practices. In most cases, say for example a GAP store, the same products can be purchased at every location anywhere in the world. Why not? Most customers who shop chains are attracted to the uniformity of a brand's offering and its attendant assurance that comes with familiar surroundings and products. Anthropologie doesn't do this. It is so confident in this no-two-stores-alike policy that it doesn't mind embracing what other stores might fear: a disappointed customer.

"Curated array" goes even deeper through other programs at Anthropologie. Its Made in Kind Program is what the company calls "a project in collaborative design." Launched in 2012, Made in Kind opened with an initial offering of eleven limited edition "capsule collections" from independent artists and designers including those who focus on sustainable materials and manufacturing processes, such as Organic by John Patrick and Samantha Peet. To drive its ethos of discovery even further, the company will invite smaller retailers to aid in buying. This opens an association between the bigger brand and cool little stores. Lost and Found, Jamie Rosenthal's two eclectic Los Angeles stores, are filled with beautiful and offbeat designs that Jamie unearths in her travels around the world. Anthropologie invited her to act as a guest buyer for a collection that would only be available in five of the chain's stores. A retailer featuring another retailer would sound almost blasphemous to those who operate a conventional store chain, but this is exactly what Anthropologie has done.

Look at the second half of Anthropologie's mission and everything fills in nicely.

"Anthropologie products are an expression of our customer's appreciation for artfulness and good design. To that end, our buyers and designers travel the world to uncover special products and to collaborate with talented artisans. Our assortment includes clothing, accessories, shoes, beauty, home furnishings, found objects, gifts and décor that exhibit influences ranging from vintage to global"

Anthropologie and Finders

In spite of all it does, Anthropologie has managed to be a pretty big brand without getting dumped by Finders. It has avoided the loss of this high value customer by setting itself up in alignment with them. Brands matter to Finders only when they connect with their values; they get rejected when they are merely brand attributes built to symbolize corporate values. When corporate and brand values equal the customer experience and the Finder's values, only then will you have a Finder brand.

Finders like to find, and this means they are usually the ones to try something new first. For a Finder, being there first isn't about status – it's about uniqueness and discovery. By exploring the world, both local and far-flung, and introducing artisans, designers, artists, guest buyers and curators, Anthropologie achieves all of this.

The real authentic is what Finders want; Anthropologie gives them that. Craftsmanship, passion, the feel of handmade, and real mastery all matter. By bringing out the "real-thing" in what it sells, Anthropologie matches Finder values and retains them by removing anything that smacks of an artificial claim of authenticity or brand before product hype.

Anthropologie isn't in the discount business. In this way, the relationship between customer and product is seldom compromised by a price argument. It is, after all, difficult to see all that value, artistry, and uniqueness in a product that, in a discounting environment, might soon be found with a big red starburst that reads, "50% OFF THIS WEEK ONLY." Finders are suspicious of discounting and Anthropologie avoids these suspicions by keeping discounts and sales events to a minimum.

It also manages to be a store for Finders and a store for Evolving Finders. The Finder, with her rich and well-exercised discretionary buying power, is the spender who occupies the bigger ticket regions of Anthropologie's product offerings. This is where the $400 shoes and the $250 dresses might be found, along with an interesting piece of art or furniture. Yet the brand also manages to fill its stores with those same Evolving Finders who power the one-off coffee shops and microbrewers of the Evolving Finder world. That means that Anthropologie's values will align with both groups. The trouble is, if any given brand were in the position to align with both Finders and Evolving Finders at the same time, the brand would only remain relevant to both by giving each group something to buy. Which is what Anthropologie does. The only buyer it doesn't court is the Keeper.

To try this idea on, let's look at a scenario where an Evolving Finder and a Keeper are both in the market for a set of soup bowls. The Keeper might decide on a look and a functional design that suits a number of factors and then go shopping in search of the best deal on that particular specification. A trip to IKEA or Walmart might yield the right deal on something that fits the bill. The Evolving Finder, on the other hand, would think in terms of design first. That shopping trip might include a poke around a few antique stores in search of the right level of originality and aesthetic, and a stop at Anthropologie where the eclectic housewares department might reveal originality in design, a story of the artisan who made the bowls, and a kind of beauty that fits the tastes of that particular Evolving Finder. The size of the purchase is already assumed to be within budget, this is confirmed with a flip of the bowl to reveal price and the Evolving Finder has completed a successful shop in the more entry-level strata of Anthropologie. Found. Bought. And Anthropologie proves itself to be a brand that can achieve alignment across 113 million Finders and Evolving Finders across America.

Anthropologie is also imperfect. The brand has been at times accused of everything from ripping off other designers to selling T-Shirts with provocative statements that have been labeled as anti-gay (ink on cotton proclamations which would require a certain level of interpretation to be seen as, at the very least, overt). But, it's up to the customer to decide what is and isn't appropriate in the retail world. Finders are generally a conscientious group; a brand that acts in a socially irresponsible way around them does so at its peril. It is enough to agree that there are certain risks that come with being a brand that does not conform to the norm. Here is where we can apply an axiom that is often heard in the art world. It seems fitting in the case of Anthropologie, and it goes like this, "If no one hates you, no one will love you either."

In the broadest terms, brands that align with Finders are successful. It is well and good to have high spending customers and a unique place in a market but business is about profit and, in retail, the common measure of such a thing is sales per square foot. Let's return to the litmus test of recession; Anthropologie managed to hold its ground through the last one very nicely. Sales during 2010 averaged a very respectable $750 per square foot as compared to an average among clothing retailers that fell to $309 per square foot. To avoid any accusations of apples and oranges comparisons, furniture and housewares retailers during this same period experienced sales levels that ranged between $166 and $240 per square foot. At $750 per square foot, Anthropologie was, by at least that measure, recession-proof.

21

◆

MASS PRODUCED ORIGINALITY

Scaling the Finder Brand

A careful look at any Finder-aligned brand and the set of qualifying factors begin to add up. Ensuring that corporate values (values at the top = values at the bottom) is most certainly no small feat and a rare accomplishment. Offering a customer experience that hits enough notes to create the ideal Finder buying environment is another. Managing to appeal and be relevant to both Finders and Evolving Finders is yet another. There is one final hurdle that applies to Anthropologie and that is perhaps the most difficult: scalability.

American business and industry has been obsessed with scale ever since Henry Ford. Since perfecting the assembly line and eventually growing into an industrial juggernaut, the concept of easily building more, has symbolized much of what is held dear to America. Size has always mattered. The inexorable loss of manufacturing jobs to China, Mexico, India, and beyond has of course created a new set of social issues and levels of unemployment that are particularly biting among those with limited educational opportunities. Perhaps this loss of manufacturing is the loss of a part of American identity and leaves us with the question, "If we don't make anything here anymore, what are we?" Yet there is still a rich and highly active market that drives the consumer economy at levels that go into the trillions of dollars every year. It would be only natural to look at Finders as a new target market and try to figure out a way to mass-produce everything a Finder might buy. Until another head shaker of a question comes up, "How do you scale unique?"

You can and you can't. In operational terms, Anthropologie has simply adjusted its product mix and created a set of product lines that are something of a blank slate. These blanks are filled in, in part, by purchases from local artisans, designer, and artists and in part by limited buys that go to a select set of stores. Yet you can walk into any Anthropologie in the world and find items that are the same across the chain. What's for sale in individual stores doesn't need to be completely different to deliver on uniqueness – it just needs to be experienced as different enough. Yes, the cliché of every snowflake being different might be true but at its core, every snowflake is still the same as the next. It's snow.

Uniqueness and originality are things that will often attract the Finder but they aren't everything. They just can't be ignored.

The Apple iPhone might be the most scalable Finder product the world has ever seen. If every human year is seven years in a dog's life, the world of technology must age in something that is at least five times faster than dog years. Thinking in those accelerated dog years might be the only way to look at the iPhone and believe that it's only been around since 2007. In that time span, the iPhone has travelled from the very leading edge of technology – a near miracle product – to something of a fixture that can be considered as everything from a tool to a bloody nuisance. With a voracious appetite for what is new and a comfort with technology, Finders were the spenders who first bought the iPhone, fell in love with it, and took it out to meet the world. Today, you will see an iPhone in the hands of many Keepers but with its top-of-the-market price, its utter lack of discounting, and continued position on the highest rung of the technology ladder, it is still the Finder's first born.

So what? What makes it unique? The flexibility of applications found on the iPhone (and indeed on its competitors' "me-too" offerings) means that everyone who owns an iPhone will choose from (as of this writing) 1.2 million applications and design their phones according to their own specifications. In this case, the iPhone is the ultimate and maybe unbeatable example of uniqueness scaled.

22

◆

THE HOUSE THAT YOGA PANTS BUILT

It was the spring of 2014 and January Jones, the actress best known for her role as Mrs. Don Draper on the TV series *Madmen*, bought herself a new home on a cul-de-sac in a nice, gated Los Angeles community. The four bedroom, five bathroom home comes in at 3,279 square feet and features a swimming pool and updated kitchen with new top-of-the-line appliances and quartz counter tops. She paid $1.7 million for this very nice but not overly showy home in an area where real estate values run among the highest in the country.

Meanwhile, on a 33 feet wide lot in Vancouver, Canada's West Side, a 2,000 square foot, 3 bedroom home, complete with vinyl siding and a slightly collapsing front porch, sat with a "FOR SALE" sign on its balding and tufted lawn. With busy traffic on the street, this "entry level old-timer" could hardly be described as a luxury executive enclave placed in an idyllic setting, but it was the only one in this 25 square mile portion of Canada's rainforest city that fit the same $1.7 million budget. Given that it was on the market for $1.698 million, it just barely squeaked in. Would that price be paid? Probably. It might in fact even go up. As is often the case in Vancouver, a bidding war may well break out.

Look for a home in Vancouver that a realtor would call a "comparable" to the one that January Jones bought, search for something with four bedrooms, five bathrooms, and about the same square footage with a new kitchen. But let's be reasonable, it would have to be a far smaller lot, forget the gated community, and a pool would be quite out of the question; in a city that gets an average of 161 days of annual rainfall, the pool wouldn't be missed much. That comparable house in Vancouver was found and priced to sell – for $3.88 million.

A few blocks away from our $1.7 million teardown sits Chip Wilson's house. No one would mistake this place for a fixer-upper. Chip's house took about five years to build. It sits on three waterfront lots. It would be reasonable to think that it has many more bedrooms and bathrooms than January's. It has a pool and one would expect that it has a kitchen stocked with appliances that are so advanced that one would imagine they could do the grocery shopping on their own. That would only make sense because with a city property tax assessment that put the value of Chip's house at an eye-watering $54 million dollars, anything seems possible.

It was a warm day in the middle of summer in 2002 when Chip Wilson sat on a flimsy chair among his fellow creditors in a rented conference room. Everyone was looking to get paid by a recently defunct Canadian sporting goods retailer with the suddenly ironic name, Superstar. Wilson hoped to collect at least part of the money owed to his newly minted yoga wear company. In the seat next to him sat the principal of a tiny advertising agency who had just lost the better part of his company's working capital and most certainly any hope of a summer vacation. A string of Superstar owners and executives sat at a head table under the protective eye of the bankruptcy trustee. Once the anger and lamentations of the creditors had washed over these former customers, buyers, borrowers, and clients for a few hours, the meeting ended with a conclusion that nothing would be distributed to anyone, at least no one sitting in that particular room. Wilson and the adman chatted sadly as the crowd filed out. Wilson said that he'd had it with retailers and was on to greener pastures. Greener pastures with what was then, nothing more than a weird name for a pair of pants that would now only be sold at Wilson's own retail stores. The name had a strange power. One that might make a person want to repeat it a few times. As in, "I love your pants, what are they?"

"Lululemon."

"Lulu-what?"

"Lululemon."

"Lululemon?"

"Right, Lululemon"

"OK then…Lululemon. Loo-loo-lemon. Huh. Weird. What

kind of company is that?"

"Yoga wear."

"Right…Yoga what?"

Here is a question. How can a yoga pant be like a Subaru? Simple. In the same way that Subaru built the definitive off-road car, Chip Wilson built the definitive yoga pant. The car and the pant were never really advertised or "branded" as such, they just were what they were; the definition of the best thing money could buy. Here's the problem. It is reasonable to expect some sort of demand for a car that can drive really well on gravel roads. After all, there are gravel roads. To further the argument in favor of an off-road car, there is something of a constant that comes in the form of complimentary products such as kayaks and cross-country skis. But how could anyone predict a future where a man with an idea for good yoga pants could become a billionaire? Where were the metaphorical gravel roads and kayaks? In other words, where was the market?

The number of yoga practitioners in the United States grew by 30% between 2008 and 2012. Today there are more than 20 million. There you have it, an unexpected proliferation of gravel roads.

Chip Wilson caught a wave made out of Finders. But to catch any wave you have to know how to surf it. Lululemon didn't look on itself as a brand that gets stitched onto a pair of pants and sold at competitive prices. It looked at itself as a set of values. Those values happened to include a determination to make the world's best yoga pant.

There are plenty of Finder businesses in this world. Yet very few ever started out with anything like an intention to be one. They got there by having qualities that happen to line up with that Finder customer. A happy accident that comes of being in the right place at the right time while, most importantly, doing the right things.

Lululemon came with a long list of right things. Some could argue it has fewer of them now than it did then. Leaving that aside for the moment, let's examine the intersections between what we can safely call a Finder company and a Finder customer. But first, let us speed toward one of those intersections and cause a bus crash.

The Problem with Real-ish

Real authenticity is power with Finders and that kind of truth-in-product is something that is easy to prove and sustain when selling one-off leather bags. As it goes with scalability there are a few ways to hold on to real authenticity. The first is, quite obviously, to keep making the best product on the market. Interestingly, Lululemon could easily be accused of failing on this count. In March of 2013, the company found itself in a much-publicized recall where it was compelled to take back its trademark pant. This was because the material had proven to be just a little too sheer for these naturally tight fitting pants. The pants, and their real and perceived tendency to reveal quite a lot more than intended on the women wearing them, became something of a hot story. Soon the "see-through" Lululemons were attracting coverage in both the mainstream press and late-night television monologues. To make matters just a little worse, this turned out to be the second product quality issue that the company had encountered that year. Earlier it had faced returns and complaints regarding color bleeding in some of its colored clothing. So what happened? Lululemon had broken the accord between its quality-first customer and the assurance of a product with a hitherto unassailable reputation. What's more, the story brought the product into a place where it wasn't looked upon so much as something carefully designed and precision crafted. Instead the vaunted Lululemon yoga pant found itself redefined as a garment that is made in pretty much the same way as any other. It wasn't an almost mystical yoga pant anymore. It had fallen to a place where it could become nothing more than an over-hyped label with a presumably cheap, presumably made-in-a-third-world-sweatshop garment attached to it.

As they do, things got worse before they got better. In a classic piece of public relations blame-storming, Lululemon told the *Wall Street Journal* that the issue came from a manufacturer and supplier that it had used since 2004. This statement landed like a collapsed headstand pose when the chief financial officer of Eclat Textile Co. of Taiwan refuted it.

"All shipments to Lululemon went through a certification

process which Lululemon had approved," Roger Lo told the newspaper. "All the pants were manufactured according to the requirements set out in the contract with Lululemon."

Online communities, bloggers, and social media turned all of this into something that was definitely not Zen. And then things got even worse. Chip Wilson is a man with an opinion. This is a quality found in most who create any GREAT BIG THING. Read Steve Job's approved biography, published posthumously, and it might have just as easily been called, "Yes It Does Take a Real Asshole to Build the Best. You're Welcome." Jobs was the embodiment of what we all love to gently call an "iconoclast." There is an old saying that must apply to a business that sticks to its convictions, "If you want to make an omelet, you have to break a few eggs." It appears that Chip Wilson is not a man who is afraid of manning the metaphorical omelet bar in support of doing and saying what he believes in.

Asked, during an interview on Bloomberg TV in the fall of 2013, what was behind Lululemon's problems with the yoga pants, Wilson admitted that the company "made a mistake" in its design, but the problem had more to do with some of the women who wore the pants. Wilson said, "The thing is that women will wear seat belts that don't work [with the pants], or they'll wear a purse that doesn't work, or quite frankly some women's bodies just actually don't work."

Issues around quality that could be pretty embarrassing for customers, a portrayal of the company's marquee offering as a brand-before-quality let-down, and finally a blatant swipe from the CEO at the gender that represents, by far, the primary share of Lululemon customers – these would surely signal the end of the Lululemon story right? Well, Probably not. We can begin with the numbers. Depending on which form of financial reporting you read (Lululemon, as a public company, changed its reporting methodology in the early months of 2014) the months that followed these 2013 pratfalls showed either a 2% rise or a 5% drop in same store sales in January 2014. But by late summer of the same year, company revenues had gone from 1.37 billion to 1.59 billion.

It is the customers who, after all, create these numbers. Interestingly, Lululemon was forgiven its sins by its customers. How could this be? The answer lies in the strength of Lululemon's relevance to Finders.

Loud and Proud Values

For almost any retailer, there is life before the Lululemon shopping bag and life after it. Up until then, shopping bags were disposable, printed with a logo, and not much else. The last retailer to do something interesting on a wide scale was Bloomingdale's with its Big Brown Bag that first appeared in 1973. Since then, not much had happened in the shopping bag business.

This Lululemon bag was very different. Ten years after its release it is fair to say that the bag is now something of a cliché.

That would almost be the point. When it hit the street during those early days it was a case of a brand wearing its heart on its sleeve (or at least on its bag). This was no accident, nor was it an overt piece of marketing. Lululemon had begun its life with what it called a manifesto, one that the company was quite happy to put right out there on its bag. To a Finder, just that manifesto on a bag seemed to line up with her values as if it came from a not quite articulated but deeply held inner belief. These were words that never broadcast a corporate agenda or attempted to gain measurable recall numbers around a slogan; they were encouragement in the form of phrases like, "do one thing a day that scares you," "the pursuit of happiness is the source of all unhappiness," "friends are more important than money," and somewhere in there, "practice yoga so you can remain active in physical sports as you age." The bags, as we all know, were a hit that might have become a little too common. By now you might see a Lululemon bag as that old, reusable lunch bag covered in gooey aphorisms. When that happens just remember that like flip cell phones and the original Oakley sunglass, anything that changes the game might be looked at with a hint of embarrassment a decade later. So go back to the early 2000s and see it for what it was, a company with Finder aligned values announced in a way that could be shared with the tribe on an eco-friendly, reusable bag. A reusable bag that has most certainly proven itself to be reused.

Product Before Price

Starbucks sells all kinds of beverages and foods but it
wouldn't be Starbucks without the coffee. Lululemon wouldn't
be Lululemon without its yoga pant. Its $98 yoga pant. On the
heels of a conversation about being out front with corporate
values comes what is probably the most important intersection
between Finder and brand: to be a winning Finder brand, the
product must be the definitive standard of quality in its category.
In yoga, in order to reach that point, the product simply has to
work best. Walk the uncluttered, bamboo floored spaces that
make up a Lululemon store and see that there are many, many
products: jackets, tops, bras, underwear, socks, headbands, water
bottles, and bags. All of them are important and all of them
help add up to the company's sales but without the pant, they
have little reason to exist. The pant in question is made with a
proprietary mix of nylon and Lycra. It is preshrunk, perfectly
stretchy, wicks away moisture, and looks pretty darn good in the
bargain. The company calls it Luon. When they were introduced
in the early days of Lululemon, the yoga pants were quite simply
the best available; they were the definitive yoga pant. Now there
is brushed Luon, reversible Luon, and heathered Luon. For a
Finder who practices yoga, there is that one yoga pant and it
is for sale at a Lululemon and who cares if it costs $98? That is
simply what it costs and that is that. Product before price.

Do a Google search on Lululemon and it won't take long to
find words of outrage against a "$100" yoga pant. Fair enough.
For a Keeper, there are cheaper pants that might not be quite

as good or might even be as good and for that reason $98 is an outrageous price. For a Keeper, at least an angry and vocal one, a $98 yoga pant seems like a good thing to rage against on the Internet. For any Keeper, angry, laid-back, or indifferent, price comes before product.

Not for Everyone – for Someone

A scroll to the bottom of a recent online news report on Lululemon could take you to the usual mix of support and trolling. One of these was rather telling. It read, "Chip Wilson is an asshole who got lucky." Is this true? Not really, in fact that might be a compliment. Of course it is absurd to relate the idea of getting "lucky" to the reality of creating an $8.4 billion company out of a pair of pants but let us dwell on the word "asshole" for a moment. Take anyone who would dare to build something so inoffensively offensive as a $98 yoga pant. Then have that same someone gather their favorite words of encouragement in one place, call the result a manifesto, and print it on a bag for all to see. Once that's done, make him an advocate for an ancient set of poses and exercises that increase well-being, vitality, and personal potential. Then give that person an opinion that not everyone agrees with and give him a platform (intended or otherwise) where his voice is in the public domain for all to hear. Then make him a billionaire. There, you have someone who isn't like everybody else and may not even be the most pleasant person who ever walked the earth – there is little evidence to support this – and you have an iconoclast, a maverick, a rebel. An asshole. It would be unrealistic to expect every yoga pant owning Finder to agree with Wilson and his ways but most would find it hard to disagree with his habit of doing things his own way. Wilson's own news blooper, that tactless equivalent of the phrase that no man should ever say, "Well, yes, your ass does look fat in those pants," got him into all kinds of trouble. (This interpretation might be troublesome in itself.) In Wilson's case, his phrase can be perceived in many ways. Let's try this: maybe Wilson was just telling it like it is, in terms of his product, therefore telling it like the product is. He didn't necessarily need to hurt a bunch of feelings to get that message across but the idea that Lululemon is for *some* people not *all* people was effectively delivered. Delivered tied to a brick perhaps, but delivered nevertheless. Maybe a version of his pants really did fail on quality, but you have to give the man a little credit for his "damn-the-bloggers-I'm-standing-by-my-yoga-pants" hubris. Did it work? Probably. But apparently it didn't work that well for Wilson. Shortly after those comments hit the news, he left the helm of the company he founded.

And for many women, no matter their shape, Lululemon was never right for them. It wasn't the quality scandals or whether they agreed with Lulu's yoga bag wisdom. It didn't matter what came out of Chip's big billionaire mouth. It wasn't even the "whole yoga thing." It was that $98 price tag.

No gravel roads, no Subarus. No yoga, no Lululemon. No yoga, no money. Those powerful discretionary spenders wouldn't be much good to Lululemon had it not been for another piece of alignment between the brand and the person: Finders are active. Get to know a canoe paddler, a kayaker, a stand-up paddle boarder, a wind surfer, a skier, a snowboarder, a hiker, a mountain biker, a trail runner, or a road biker and there is a better than average chance that you will meet someone who cares more about the quality of time spent than the quantity of money paid. Yoga brings peace of mind and is a route to better personal performance in sports, and in all kinds of life activities. Yoga has met its confirmed practitioner in the world of Finders.

The Store That Chip Built

Then there was that warm day in 2002 when Chip Wilson counted himself among those who had come to pick over the remains of a failed sporting goods retailer. That was a day when Wilson said he was going to do things differently. He had already opened his own store a few years earlier but, at the time, that one location was just another distribution channel.

Once, things were different – but this almost goes without saying. You can't buy Lululemon in the athletic section of a Walmart or a Target. You can't buy Lululemon in a sporting goods store. You can't even buy it in a yoga store. Not anymore at least.

In 2002, Chip Wilson began to take over 100% of the environment where his product would be sold. From that point on, Lululemon could only be bought in a store called Lululemon.

That decision did not come of getting paid or not getting paid. It came of control.

What made that move so visionary can really only be illustrated by looking at a non-existent parallel universe. Let's call it, "Lululemon the mass-retail brand." Visit this imaginary universe to see the iconic yoga pant as it rides home from someone else's store in someone else's bag. Cringe at the sight of a yoga-friendly sports bra as it is sold to a 40-year-old mom by a 17-year-old skater dude with "Jeff" printed on his sporting goods superstore nametag. Then wonder where it all went so wrong as you spy a dusty Lululemon jacket as it swings from the end of a long clearance rack at TJ Max.

It's all 20/20 hindsight, but this time hindsight doesn't show the mistakes, it shows the bloody genius of a decision that moved all of Wilson's products into his own exclusive retail environment.

Finally, it is more than safe to say that by controlling the environment Lululemon saved itself from a fate that would have taken it far from the Finder's world.

Lululemon is a strong Finder brand. It is one that intersects with many Finder attributes including product before price, matching values, a definitive position as the finest product, and a personality that marches to its own drummer. They all count, but there is a recurring theme around Lululemon that can be found in many Finder-aligned companies and it takes us back to Wilson. Lululemon's "lulululemon-ness" came from the leadership of a strong personality.

Jim Collins' 1991 classic, *Good to Great: Why Some Companies Make the Leap and Others Don't* speaks of the dangers of a company built around a single personality. Collins quite correctly asserts that any company built under such a structure contains a self-destructive flaw. Once that single key personality leaves, whatever the circumstances, the company becomes vulnerable to any number of threats, both internal and external. Collins covers even more ground in his book when he makes a point that can resonate with any Finder business. He reports that organizations with longevity and long-term success have been found to show a strong set of internal values. These are values that are put into action and held sacred above any short-term thinking that might be used in the pursuit of short-term financial gain. To go by *Good to Great* is to spot a threat on the horizon for Lululemon.

23

◆

THE FIGUREHEAD AND THE CORPOROCRAT

Lululemon might not be everything it once was – in fact it isn't. The person who controls the financial future of the company, its culture, its values, its store environments, and of course its products isn't a surfer-ish yoga dude with a habit of speaking his mind. It isn't even his new self, a billionaire who lives in a really nice house in a really nice neighborhood in a really expensive city. Lululemon has been a public company for a number of years, and it has been quite some time since Chip Wilson flew solo. Lululemon's former CEO, Christine Day, saw the company through its greatest time of growth and new CEO, Laurent Potdevin, has the makings of a fine replacement. Yet without an ultimate leader – which Chip Wilson was, first as entrepreneur and finally as Chairman, a Finder brand runs the risk of losing its best customer. This is because when a company goes public a CEO isn't really in a place of ultimate power. Neither is the President, the CMO, the CFO, or the COO. In a public company the buck ultimately stops with one entity: the owner. And it is here that a Finder company can encounter its worst kind of owner, the shareholder.

There are few if any examples of a shareholder who cares about the fit of a pair of pants much less the empowerment of a customer through encouragement and a strong, vital mind and body. The shareholder doesn't often care about how happy employees are or the carbon footprint of a retail store; the shareholder cares about money. Money and the job that money does when it creates return on investment, impact on share value, quarterly performance, and dividends. The Shareholder does not look ahead with vision; the shareholder looks at the numbers today. Don't blame the average hard-working, money-saving Keeper for this one but, not coincidentally, the Shareholder can be seen as the ultimate manifestation of price before product.

Shareholders, through their boards and then through upper management, have a natural attraction to others who care about share values, dividends, and quarterly performance. They care so much in fact that those are the usual metrics around performance bonuses and salary calculations for those who run the show at publicly owned companies.

Finders Run Finder Companies for Finder Customers

In Wilson's case, and in the case of all of those microbrewers, Swiss courier bag magnates, and even the ubiquitous Starbucks Coffee, a fact is brought to the surface again and again. Finder businesses must have Finder customers and the only way to do that is to have Finders leading them and running them.

In 2014, the Canadian news weekly, *Maclean's* reported that Wilson was working to try and regain control of the company he founded and, if we're fair, cashed out on. In June of 2014, Wilson announced that he would use his 27 percent stake in the company to fight the re-election of two board members: one a former Starbucks executive and the other the president of a private equity firm. It is true that Wilson had left the company shortly after his foot-in-mouth comments of 2013, but that June he made it quite clear that he was not prepared to let go just yet. For good reason. In a quote pulled by *Maclean's* from a myriad of customer comments was this telling piece:

> *"I'm losing my allegiance to the only brand of athletic wear I felt I had a personal relationship with," wrote one user. In June, in response to a post showcasing looser-fitting patterned summerwear, an effort to sell its athletic gear as street fashion, customers were incensed: "Lulu was special because it had it all – great beautiful designs, high-quality fabrics, wonderful figure-flattering fits. No more."*

Wilson seemed to be coming to the rescue as he waded into this fight with a warning that these re-elections would mean a Lululemon that would sacrifice "product, culture, and brand and longer-term corporate goals" for "short-term results."

The fracas didn't last. By June of 2015, Wilson had thrown in the towel, selling his remaining shares in the company to a private equity firm. Active and yoga-devoted Finders of the world can only hope that he had made his point.

There are reasons to feel positive about Lululemon's future. Former Tom's Shoes CEO, Laurent Potdevin, was hired in 2013 as Christine Day's replacement. As of this writing it appears that in Potdevin, Lululemon has a Finder in the CEO seat. His resume certainly reads that way with career stops at other category-definitive companies like snowboard and apparel brand, Burton and a track record of socially conscious work at that Finder favorite, Tom's Shoes. There might just be one problem. In the press and online, Potdevin, with his less than beach-ready-body, has been branded "Lululemon's dumpy new CEO." No Potdevin doesn't do yoga.

24

WHEN HARRY MET STARBUCKS

A Romantic Tragicomedy

Chip Wilson was not the first and will certainly not be the last creator of Finder greatness to catch a case of the post-sale blues. Worse, those blues will inevitably find their way to the customer.

Which brings up Starbucks. Starbucks might be the perfect case study for what we can call the failed corporatization of a Finder company. It is a story that reads like a classic three-act movie script. A kind of boy-meets-girl, boy-loses-girl, boy-gets-girl-back-again arc where "boy" is replaced by "brand" and "girl" is replaced by "Finder." Get out your popcorn because here it is ladies and gentlemen, Starbucks, a brand-gets-Finder, brand-loses-Finder, brand-gets-Finder-back-again story.

Starbucks began life in the 1970s in Seattle's Pike Place Market as that perfect spot to discover what real coffee drinking should be all about. With their funky interiors decorated with coffee bags and assorted roasting paraphernalia, their cool music, the whistles and clanks of the large espresso machines, the strong scent of newly roasted beans and freshly brewed coffee, Starbucks had the environment nailed. Then came the showmanship of those who performed the act of a seemingly newly coined job description, the "barista." Finally, there came a cup of coffee from an entirely different world than that of the standard domestic dishwater. If you're old enough, you might remember that even the name was kind of fun to say. These little shops were a perfect blend of sound, smells, theatre, and an absolutely definitive product. Finder nirvana.

By the late eighties, Starbucks had become a phenomenon. Getting a Starbucks was suddenly something that put a town on the map. Interestingly, its fast ascent into our consciousness came with the sound of two kinds of comments – comments that separated two kinds of people. A comment from one kind of consumer might have been, "I love this place, I love this cappuccino!" And another from another kind of consumer would be, "Five dollars for a coffee? What, are you nuts?" Starbucks in those early days might have been as strong an indicator between Finder and Keeper as anything in the world.

Boy had met girl. Brand had met Finder. If one were to look at what was the actual "person part of the boy" one would meet another leader with the vision to bring a definitive product to people in an environment that filled the senses and never stinted on quality in the aim of a low price. That person was Howard Schultz.

Anyone who has sat through a romantic comedy knows what happens in the second act. So here's how it went for Starbucks. The brand moved from individualized stores with comfortable, sensory-loaded environments found on the better city street corners, and moved into cookie cutter drive-thrus perched on every strip mall, in every town, in every place, everywhere. In a rush to serve what suddenly seemed like an insatiable demand, the wildly successful and profitable company began to stack compromise upon compromise. Starbucks had taken the idea of creating a "third place," a cool environment somewhere between being at home and being at work, and turned it into "that generic place." One morning the boy woke up and the girl was gone.

It was time to do what the hero always does in these movies. Deep introspection was needed to figure out where he went wrong. It is here where we cue the music and play the vignette-framed flashback sequence. Start with the upbeat and cute moments as Starbucks explodes into an under-caffeinated world. Then play some minor-key strings as we watch a gauze-filtered memory of something lost between Pike Place Market and a green Formica kiosk bolted into a tattered old Safeway. Starbucks had lost its soul. It had also lost Howard Schultz.

Where had it all gone so wrong? The company had done the inevitable and gone public. Then it replaced its founder with a former Pepsi executive who exhibited some distinctly Keeper qualities. It was simply a matter of time before the originality, sensory stimulation, and theatre of a Starbucks was replaced by cookie cutter, ersatz coffeehouse, linoleum-lined stores equipped with monolithic and robotic automatic barista machines. The rich, sensory arousing scent of fresh roasted coffee had been sealed inside more efficient and inventory-control-friendly vacuum packed bags.

The girl packed her toothbrush and went home. Or, in this case, the chain lost most of its high margin, complex coffee-buying Finder customers to one-off cappuccino bars that did a better job of offering that sensory-loaded space and that definitive cup of caffeine. Now any one of over 21,000 worldwide Starbucks locations could be found with lines of $1-a-cup-buying Keepers. That meant that Starbucks was soon forced to compete on something it had never really considered, price. Once price became a driver, Starbucks found itself up against a stack of late entering commoditizers like McDonald's. The commoditizers came to the party armed with pre-mixes and behind-counter machinery that manufacture something that approximates that once definitive Starbucks latte and cappuccino. In its rush from product-first concept to global brand, Starbucks had taken a few wrong turns and found itself in a Keepers world. Now, in a strange plot twist, Starbucks found itself in competition with the cheap Styrofoam cups from ampm and Dunkin' Donuts that it had rendered obsolete all those years ago.

What happened? There is much to be learned in Howard Schultz's 1999 book, *Pour Your Heart Into It: How Starbucks Built a Company One Cup at a Time.* Far more can be gleaned from his

2012 book, *Onward: How Starbucks Fought for Its Life without Losing Its Soul.* An apt title and one that he had likely been thinking about back in 2007 when he wrote a much leaked email to senior Starbucks executives lamenting the "commoditization of the Starbucks experience" and the loss of the "romance and theatre" of its noisy, lively baristas. By 2008, Schultz was back in charge. Soon after that the robot machines were out, the scent-killing seals were off the coffee bags and average sales were way up with the slow but steady return of a cappuccino and latte drinking Finder customer, the one who had adopted the green mermaid in the first place. Yes, the boy had won the girl back. We can now roll the credits over an epilogue that would make even the dreaded Finder-repelling investor walk out of the theatre with an ear-to-ear grin. Since Schultz's return, share prices have tripled in value.

Together in Imperfect Harmony

Starbucks gets both Finders and Keepers. Does this mean that success can be found on that middle territory between the two kinds of spenders? Can a Finder company be a Keeper company too? The answer is, yes, but.

Starbucks, through its ubiquity has put itself in a rather unique position. It is one that most companies had best avoid. On any given day, in any given Starbucks lineup, there will be both Finder and Keeper. In 2014, the average purchase at a Starbucks was $7.01. The average purchase at an independent coffee shop came in significantly higher at $8.43. Those independent coffee shops, the ones that serve that unique experience to a Finder-heavy audience, get to enjoy a higher average sale because they don't have a price-sensitive customer. So does Starbucks. But Starbucks has another kind of customer in its mix and it's one that buys a lower priced offering in the form of plain old coffee. It's about two bucks a cup. This is how Starbucks has developed a split personality. On one side it has a customer that is still in search of that definitive product in an espresso bar drink and is happy to pay for it; but this customer doesn't really take Starbucks seriously and will often go to the more authentic feeling place next door. With over 21,000 locations, Starbucks will still get that customer. It may no longer be the first choice though – it's just the one that happens to be on the nearest corner.

Then there is that other customer. This is a customer that embodies a much stronger attraction to the big brand. And Starbucks is just that. According to Interbrand's 2013 international Top 100 brand value rankings, Starbucks comes in at number ninety-one, just above Heineken and right below Chevrolet. So, as the solid brand that sells coffee, coffee that starts at around $2.00, Starbucks fits the Keeper's world quite nicely. Good news? Not quite. This is where the "but" comes in; that Keeper has also been heading to McDonald's and other price-first brands for a cup of price-before-product coffee. Even with all that competition, through sheer numbers it's hard to miss a Starbucks. Now for just a bit more "but." Starbucks is a classic case of the exception that proves a rule. It does business with both Finders and Keepers and by doing so flirts with a particular danger. It is falling into middle ground. On one side of the coffee equation are Finders. Their first coffee choice is a one-off coffee joint where they might not even think about the $8 that they're dropping. On the other is the Keeper who can be perfectly satisfied with a $1.00 coffee at McDonald's. And in the middle, in a place where it does not represent an ideal coffee buying experience for either Finder or Keeper, sits Starbucks.

To finally answer the question, "Can a Finder company be a Keeper company too?" The answer is, yes, but ultimately, no.

25

◆

THEY DON'T CALL IT NO MAN'S LAND FOR NOTHING

Let's travel to another life. While we're at it, let's go back in time. You can be the star. In this life it is the mid eighties and you have a store that sells small household appliances and vacuum cleaners. Now we will give you a name and a gender. You're a nice, hard-working, and smart guy. We'll call you Bob. Hello Bob. You were going to name your store after yourself but Bob's Appliances was taken by another Bob so, after a few tries, you land on Super Bob's Appliance Center. Times are good and soon you open another store. Then another. One day a bright manager approaches you and asks if he can open another SBAC in the next town. Time goes by, a decade or two pass. You wake up one day and there are sixty SBACs across eleven states. Way to go Bob. You have created a regional brand. This really is a great country. It is only a matter of time before you go nationwide.

Your stores are known for their expert service, a near-legendary, no-questions-asked return policy, and, with attention to nice lighting and comfortable spaces, your stores have a nice vibe to them. During certain times of the year you'll have a sale but, for the most part, the tag on that blender, mixer, or toaster is the manufacturer's suggested retail price. You have a loyal customer base. Your employees are well trained, you pay them well, and you offer them a solid medical plan.

Wait. You just broke character. You're shaking your head? Yes, you already know where this story is going don't you? Let's accelerate the process with a multiple-choice quiz.

You are about to go out of business because:

a) Decades of technological advancements and offshore production turn everything that you sell into a commodity so that few care enough about your small appliances to be loyal to you.

b) The Internet makes it possible to get consumer reviews and advice on everything you sell, making the need for well-trained staff and the importance of them to the customer irrelevant.

c) Walmart comes to one of your markets, and then another, and so on. It offers the lowest prices. No one cares enough about service to overcome a price difference that sits at about 30%.

d) You respond to the Walmart challenge by offering to beat their pricing, in spite of the gulf between the two of you in buying power. At the same time, you try to offer that same high level of service in that same feel-good shopping environment.

You guessed it – there are no wrong answers.

Super Bob's Appliance Center, your once-proud business, is a broad example of a business that got caught in the middle of an industry that was driven into commoditization. Finders and Keepers alike stopped caring about any discernable differences between your products, both physical and service related, making them a commodity to be purchased at the lowest price. The battlefield moved and you got caught in no-man's land. Sorry about that Bob.

This is the story of Circuit City who was the second largest appliance retailer in America after Sears. This is also the story of Linens N Things, The Bombay Company, and hundreds of businesses that disappeared during, before, and after the recession. The reasons for their demise are often spoken of in terms of bad management, poor financing, and, in the case of your imaginary chain of appliance stores, and of course in the case of Blockbuster Video, obsolescence. Yet there is another reason for failure that lies underneath all of those sad stories of lost jobs and dreams: companies that fail often do so by getting caught between being a Finder business and a Keeper business. This can be illustrated quite simply by using just one element of what separates Finders from Keepers, product and price. There is simply no such thing as "product before price before product" or "price before product before price." One simply cannot have it both ways.

26

◆

THE THREAD COUNT OF DOOM

Linens N Things

In 2005, bedding retailer, Linens N Things reported revenues of $2.70 billion. By the end of 2008, the stores had ceased to exist.

There was a time when you could buy a set of sheets and pillowcases at a few places in any town. Perhaps there would be a bedding shop somewhere selling duvets and comforters and, of course, there would be a department store where a fitted sheet could be bought during the same trip that might yield a few pairs of socks or a new skirt.

Then things changed. If you were to leave the planet during that time, say on some kind of space mission, then return a decade later it would be easy to assume that the world had become a place where every living being was required to own at least a dozen sheet sets. Each. What other plausible explanation could there be for the promotion of a category from some little shop on main street to a set of warehouse mega stores called Linen's n Things and Bed Bath & Beyond. To be fair, Bed Bath

& Beyond has the "bath" and "beyond" related products for sale to undoubtedly mitigate the seeming excess of that brand's very existence. You still have to wonder where that same warehouse-store-at-every-other-mall need for "bath" came from but let's leave that aside before we are forced to move on to what "beyond" means.

Bed linens contain some interesting borders between Finders and Keepers. Anyone who has spent an uncomfortable night between non-breathable, itchy, or pilled sheets would agree that bedding is a sensory purchase. One can live with a cheap barbecue that sort of barbecues or a microwave that sort of cooks. Nobody wants to sleep on sheets that are so cheap that they feel like a set of itchy trash bags. Does this mean that sheets cannot be commoditized? Far from it. There is commoditization but it comes from a strange measurement, one that's in play during any sheet and pillowcase purchase. It wasn't a common term when you went on that space mission. It is now. It's called thread count.

Thread count is simply a piece of data but it has a strange power. It provides a specific measurable that is, at least perceived by the customer, to be a reliable constant when looking at the quality of bed sheets. Before the thread count there was only really one way to buy bed sheets. Go to the store, talk to somebody who knows about sheets, get some advice and some input, get to the sheets you like, and make a decision based on quality and budget. Generally speaking, sheets don't come with a money-back guarantee. That makes them the sort of medium level purchase that you would want to get right the first time.

Thread count as a measurement just means the number of threads that are woven together per square inch of fabric. If you were to take a very (very) loose weave of 50 threads, woven across another 50 threads in a square inch you would calculate the thread count by adding the two together. In this case, your thread count would be 50 + 50 = 100.

A constant measurable, even if it's only a perceived one, is a very good way to take a qualitative measurement and make it quantitative. That is, if you were to look at the price of gasoline, putting aside octane levels for the moment, the only measureable would be the volume measurement that it is sold by and the price – how much per gallon. Gas wouldn't be priced by a qualitative such as color or scent – only volume. Extend this kind of measurement process to bed sheets sold at cost per thread count and you can see how the application of a quantitative measurement to what was once considered a consultative, qualitative process creates a commodity.

The first one to popularize this sort of measurement in any industry has much to gain. This means that in the case of bedding a large portion of the sales mix could be made automatic. It goes something like this, tell the customer what a good thread count is on a good material, (in the case of bed sheets, generally it's Egyptian cotton). Then apply a price, one that is usually framed as a sale price. There you have it, sales simplified and a newly educated customer who perceives, through this new measurement, that a better sleep can be bought at a specific price.

It was as if one simple metric had provided a flood of new customers for the sleeps sets at Linens N Things and enough of them to share with Bed Bath & Beyond and the like. And with it came a problem. Let's return to the gas analogy for a moment. Gas stations, when business is off, will get into a price war. It doesn't seem to happen as often as it did in the past but let's try it on. Gas Station A is having a rough week. Gas Station B, sitting there on the opposite corner, is too. So Gas Station A decides to lower its price per gallon by five cents. Soon a line of cars forms at its pumps while the pumps at Gas Station B are left empty. Then Gas Station B counters with a further five cent cut and the line moves across the street. The two stations continue to lower prices until one of them (or both) starts to lose too much money and stops the madness. Peace and higher prices return.

Now substitute Gas Station A and Gas Station B for Linens N Things and Bed Bath & Beyond; substitute opposite corner for opposite strip mall (or "power center"); then swap out price per gallon for price per thread count and you have a race to the bottom of pricing and profit that the price-sensitive customer benefits from. Only in this case a price war leaves permanent damage. When it comes to those competing gas stations, there is always the expectation among customers that prices will travel upward after a price war. Then there will be other fluctuations where prices move up and down (usually up) with supply and market forces.

Bed sheets are different. Once prices have been driven down by increasingly aggressive sales events, they don't recover in perceived value. Instead, a benchmark is set in the minds of consumers that sits somewhere around the lowest sale price. By promoting and selling on thread count, Linens N Things and Bed Bath & Beyond created a monster. They took a crucial part of their sales mix and commoditized it. Worse yet, unlike a gas station that requires a huge fixed asset in the form of land and equipment, plus the licensing and franchising fees (or oil company ownership), almost any retailer can stock sheets and put them on sale using that same cost/thread count constant. If you want to sell gas, there's a huge barrier to entry. If you want to sell 400 thread count Egyptian cotton sheets, there's some shelf space in Aisle 4.

When a business, or even a large portion of a sales mix, is driven to commoditization life can be fleeting and somebody usually gets killed off. By 2008, the one-day-only-discount reaper had done his thing at Linens N Things and the company had ceased to exist in bricks and mortar form. They still do business; you can buy from them right now, presumably by the thread count, but only online. Which makes sense because with that kind of no-brainer commodity, who needs a store?

Those of you who are reading this and know a little more about bedding can now relax. The Linens N Things thread count quantifier commoditization conundrum is built on a flawed concept. Thread count isn't necessarily the mark of a good sheet. But for a Keeper looking to get as much (highest thread count) for as little as possible (on sale now for a low price) the whole thread count thing is a godsend. It still is. Want a deal on a set of sheets? You will find it and it will always be expressed in the same terms, thread count and cost.

If you are a Finder, you might do the same. We have, after all, created a commodity with little if any discernable differences between most products with the exception of price. Finders will dig deeper, seek more information, and look for the story. Yes, there is a Finder bed sheet. It is sold by that same person who was there when the story started – the one who knows that thread count is one of many marks of a good sheet but not the defining one. There is material, type of weave, source of the material, and a whole set of qualities that go into making that perfect sleeping envelope. You just have to do what a Finder does. Find it.

In the end, Linens N Things was doomed by what is a constant for failure in so many businesses. It could not profitably deliver the lowest price on what it helped commoditize so it could not win a stable place in the world of the Keeper. Furthermore, by neglecting to offer informative service, engaging environments, and any kind of aligned values, and positioning itself as a price-before-product brand, it could not attract or gain loyalty among a high margin Finder customer. Linen N Things couldn't give either Finders or Keepers what they wanted so it died a lonely death without either of them at its side.

27

STUCK IN THE MIDDLE WITHOUT YOU

The Bombay Company

The Bombay Company started out life as a mail order company that advertised in high-end magazines and ended up on life support in a Fred Meyer grocery store. There you have the short version of what was, in 2004, a 500-store retail chain that occupied about 400 malls and 100 stand-alone locations across the U.S. and Canada.

To read the history of The Bombay Company is to learn the story of a company that went through more than a few ups and downs over a twenty-odd year timeline. When expressed in terms of profitability, a graph of the company's financials would look like a half submerged porthole on a storm-tossed sea. The times that The Bombay Company could be seen to be riding the top of the profit wave are significant and highly indicative.

The Bombay Company began life as a mail-order seller of exotic looking knock-offs of trendy and upscale looking tables and furnishings. Those early days are less relevant here so let's pick up the story in 1980 when The Bombay Company was sold to Canadian entrepreneur Robert Norse. Once he'd written the check and set to work, Norse did three things right. First, he invested heavily in the design of the first store and opened it in the busiest mall in Toronto, Ontario – North America's fourth largest city. By doing so he created an environment that felt like a fashion store, but one that sold furniture. Then he made the company's own brand designs easily affordable. Next, he stuck with the brand's original mail-order shipping format so that he could stock most items as flat packs in store and offer instant take-home gratification to shoppers. The formula worked and before long Bombay Company locations were popping up across North America. The company enjoyed success, at least for a time. Then along came Ikea to dominate the flat-pack furniture business. Then higher-end competitors appeared on the scene to take ownership of a premium position that aligned more closely with Norse's original furniture-as-fashion ethic. By the early nineties, the company had a new majority owner and was losing money. This was just the first time that The Bombay Company would find itself caught between the poles of low price/cheaply made and premium priced/great looking/built to last.

The Bombay Company fought back. Surprisingly, they won. With a new design-first esthetic and its own designed and manufactured products that were sold in stores at premium prices, the furniture retailer enjoyed resurgence. It was something of a renaissance that The Bombay Company enjoyed during the high times that began around the end of the Reagan administration in the late eighties, then carried through Bush Senior and into the Clinton years of the early nineties. It was during those heady days that the company grew to 500 stores. It created the offshoots Alex & Ivy and later Bombay Kids. Yes, The Bombay Company was winning with a customer who was there for the product and not the price. With well designed stores, total control over the quality and design of its products, and strong locations the company had successfully fought its way out of the middle ground and into Finder world. These were good times. With a strong balance sheet and a clear outlook, The Bombay Company made the bold move out of the mall and into stand-alone large format stores.

That could be where the trouble began. At about 1,200 square feet each, a shopping mall Bombay Company store was an intimate space with something of an eclectic and bountiful offering. It could get a little crowded but that was part of the charm. Now, with stand-alone stores measuring in at over 4,000 square feet, there just wasn't enough interesting inventory to fill the space. Too much dead air. And too few customers. There had to be a solution and it had to come quickly. The Bombay Company hit the ground running with two new strategies; they would both prove to be malignant.

First came a rush to acquire more merchandise to fill up those big stores. Smart and thoughtful buying took a back seat to quantity over quality. But at least the big stores wouldn't ring with that empty echo anymore. Once a near-acceptable level of volume had been achieved inside the big stores, it was time to put the same SKUs into the smaller stores. After all, it seemed important to have the same goods for sale across all locations.

Right? Once The Bombay Company had created that constant offering across all formats, it had completed its first strategic mistake. Mall locations went from charmingly eclectic to just plain messy and overstocked. Meanwhile, those bigger stores were now just barely full but the condition of "almost enough" wasn't due to new and interesting items worth discovering and paying for; the stores were burdened with low-quality, hastily-built, and poorly designed pieces. It wasn't furniture, it was filler.

Then came the second strategy and this one was even more reactive. No company lives in a vacuum. The nineties were bookended by two recessions. The first was the short-term recession that probably ended George Bush Sr's one-term stint in the oval office. It was the one that gave Clinton's camp that great one-liner, "It's the economy, stupid." The second recession came toward the end of that decade with the burst of the dot-com bubble.

With each of these recessions, The Bombay Company responded by lowering its prices and, simultaneously, its product quality. These moves came with what sounded like a sensible rationale, "make the stores more accessible and more affordable."

At the end of the eighties, The Bombay Company had reached its height of popularity and profitability as a brand-unto-itself. It built that brand by selling its own kind of interesting, original, and not over-priced, but also not discounted, goods in cool environments. By the end of the next decade what had made the brand special had been ground away by poor location strategies, reactive band-aid solutions and a lack of confidence in the staying power of its customer. The Bombay Company had become a mass merchandiser of near-discount furniture that was no longer so very different from anything else on the market. It wasn't a Finder's store anymore. It had never really made it as a Keeper store either. It had become just another purveyor of mediocrity stumbling into the next decade with no particular customer, dying a slow death somewhere in the middle.

The Canadian and American versions of Bombay Company parted ways in 2007, shortly before the bankruptcy of the U.S. division. The Canadian version called it quits in 2014.

Yet it is not over for this brand. Not quite. In 2008, the parent company to Crate & Barrel, Hermes-OTTO International, acquired the master license for Bombay Company. Today, you can find certain items from The Bombay Company product line revived and sold, like the remnants of Linens N Things, though a number of non-bricks and mortar channels including television-shopping channel QVC.

In 2012, grocery chain Fred Meyer began selling select Bombay Company branded pieces at 116 stores in Alaska, Idaho, Oregon, and Washington. Furniture sold at a grocery chain that carries the brand slogan, "Save time, money and gas.®" Perhaps today there is new life for what is left of The Bombay Company, but likely in brand name only and sold with a Keeper's price tag.

28

◆

BREAKDOWN ON KEEPER STREET

Panic in Detroit

It would be easy to look at companies that went bankrupt and disappeared over the past few years, give a self-satisfied shrug, say something about survival of the fittest, and move on. This simply wouldn't tell the story. Everything is not peachy for those that made it through to sell another day.

In 2008, the United States Treasury Department took temporary control of what had once been the biggest carmaker in the world, General Motors. When a carmaker with cars featured in more than a few Bruce Springsteen songs finds itself in the financial palliative care unit, you know the world has turned itself upside down. Back in 2008, even Chevrolet – the brand representing the third leg of America's apple-pie, baseball, and Chevrolet national identity trio – was on government-funded life support. Barn-mates Oldsmobile, Buick, GMC, Cadillac, Hummer, Saturn, and even misbehaving Swedish stepchild Saab were being wheeled to the morgue. General Motors, as we all know, was bailed out to the tune of $80 billion by the U.S. taxpayer. For a time, it was fashionable among cynics and fatalists to call GM, "Government Motors." Since 2008, GM's U.S. dealer network has dropped from over 6,300 locations to 4,355. That is probably a good thing.

Let's begin with the usual diagnosis, one that points out that GM was a victim of a precipitous drop in customer spending combined with a severe credit crunch. It's not wrong, but it is only partly correct. It overlooks some things and oversimplifies others. General Motors had an overextended dealer network, one that stood as a holdover from the days of dominant market share. Then there were the customer satisfaction issues that had dogged the brand since the 1970s. Relentless foreign competition had shadowed GM since gaining a foothold in that same decade. Combine the negative forces brought on by the recession with the vulnerabilities that had already taken hold and GM was a sitting duck. All true. All relevant. Yes. All of the answer? No. At tracking the heart of it all, GM had lost its customer.

It is hard to say when it happened. All that can be said is that one day a Chevrolet or even a Cadillac was not the car everybody wanted anymore. Many point to the first energy crisis of the 1970s when Detroit struggled to make a lighter, more fuel-efficient car. One might remember them: the Ford Pinto, the Chrysler K Cars, the Chevy Vega, and the Chevrolet Citation. They were a hurried response to soaring oil prices and superior technology, efficiency, and reliability of the imports. All of them were terrible. GM, with its dominant market share, might not have made the worst car. Anyone who has ever owned an AMC Gremlin would certainly agree. Instead, "The General" won the terrible race on pure volume; GM sold more terrible Vegas than Ford sold terrible Pintos than Chrysler sold terrible, well, everything. Everybody lost. Customers began to disappear, leaving the big three American automakers and their numerous, powerful, and fast-sinking dealer networks with perhaps one option, the sale. It's hard to say why, but it would seem that once Detroit went on sale back in 1972, it never stopped. Let's travel to present day and look back. Try to remember a day in living memory when an American car wasn't on sale.

Imagine a product – a good product that has a lot of great features and carries a lot of innovative technology. Maybe it receives critical praise from magazines and testing bodies in its industry. Maybe it has a great warranty. Now take that product and stick a huge red sale sticker on each and every one that you sell; the customer has to wonder what the catch is. The customer on some level might wonder why, if this product is so great, it needs help getting out the door. It is the sale sticker that tends to obscure anything else that is great about the product.

That is precisely what car manufacturers do.

It is difficult to turn on a television anywhere in America, open a paper, surf a site, or listen to a radio without hearing THE GREAT AMERICAN CAR COMMERCIAL. The one that extolls a long list of standard features, points out some sort of critical praise, and hits hard on a price offer. If it's a radio spot for a truck, the announcer speaks in a voice that sounds like gunpowder, red meat, and chainsaw oil. If it's a TV spot for an entry-level car, it's a pop video with upbeat music and a cast of generically attractive and ethnically ambiguous young people. Luxury car – white man, tuxedo, excellent bone structure, better yet, a celebrity. The content is always the same.

For the sake of comparison, let us now take that darling Finder brand, Apple, and give it the American Car Company commercial treatment.

MUSIC: Upbeat, contemporary, female singer, light hip feel.

ANNCR: It's wowed the critics all over the world, with sleek European inspired aluminum styling and lightning fast processing speed. The award winning Apple MacBook is the laptop computer that everybody's talking about.

SING: Yeah!

ANNCR: Now get in to your Apple dealer and get the 500 gig solid-state hard drive that the competition can't touch. And get $200 dollars off when you come in now!

SING: Apple!

ANNCR: Apple. Future! Dependable! Value!

```
Then let us support this factory campaign with a
dealer commercial.

PHIL:      Crazy Phil here for Crazy Phil's Apple
           Megastore! Folks, you have got to get
           down here right now because the deals
           on Macs are ROCK BOTTOM-BOTTOM-BOTTOM
           (insert echo effect here).
           That's right because it's our year-end
           clearance and these Macs have got to go
           so prices are craaaaazzzzzyyyy!
```

Are you having a tough time imagining a world where an Apple store might stoop to such a thing? It wouldn't need to right? After all, sales per square foot at an Apple store are a record-holding $4,551 per square foot. You'd have to wonder if things would be better, more Apple-like perhaps – for Ford, or GM, or Chrysler if they didn't advertise at all? Or at least not in this way.

There is much to like about the cars that come out of Detroit these days. Unfortunately, they are products that are hidden behind a price tag. A price tag exhaustively supported with advertising.

When handing out the blame for a price-before-product car industry, one can quickly run out of fingers to point. There are the dealers. By the recession they had already suffered through decades of being saddled with poor design and bad ideas from the factory. Again, there are 4,355 GM dealerships in America today. Market share fell to its lowest in 2012 at 17.9%. Compare that to Toyota's 14.3% 2012 market share and that doesn't seem too bad, that is until you account for the fact that with only around 1,200 dealerships across the country, every Toyota dealer sells more cars.

Take too many car dealers with too few cars sold and price-cutting advertising will always ensue. It is advertising that is generated at the factory level, fueled in no small part by pressure from a dealer group. It isn't fair to blame it all on the dealers, they are simply living on the battlefront. Short term sales feel good at all levels where success is measured by sales per month and per quarter (and executive remuneration is often calculated on a similar metric). Then comes the price-cutting advertising from the dealer level, which gets increasingly shrill as too many retailers fight for those too few customers. It is only natural that advertising used during such times should smack of a certain sort of short-term thinking. What person in this position would want to build a brand relationship based on something as airy and granola as a set of real values or a well-demonstrated show of product superiority? Inevitably, the one-way conversation from dealer to disinterested customer gets to be about the deal. In advertising, the deal means this: stuff a lot of features in, find some authority in the form of third party endorsements – no matter how tenuous ("the critics are raving") – then badger your audience. Voila, a few customers show up, the kind of customer who only lives for the deal, and suddenly there's a little food in the starving showroom. Then do it again. And again.

It is this kind of short-term solution that moves any brand into the land of the Keeper.

Now let's test the Keeper factor with a bit of a score sheet. The car business provides a great example, or you can put yourself in the shoes of almost any business, including your own, and see what comes out the other end. Answer the following questions:

a) Is this brand's usual way of getting customers based on offering a short-term discount?

b) Are your products sold by extolling a long list of features that aren't unique to you but common to your industry? For example, video interface, safety rating, ABS.

c) Does your brand depend on authority, such as critical reviews, or celebrity endorsements to add credibility to your claims?

d) Is your product trying to be like someone else's instead of other products that try to be like yours? In other words, are you building a car to compete with, for example, BMW instead of BMW building a car to compete with you?

e) Are you leaning on your brand's claims, values, slogans, jingles, and "image" more than your actual product?

f) Are you trying to advertise your way out of trouble?

GM gets 100% on this particular quiz. This makes life very

difficult for the brand. Life as a Keeper brand means always being stuck in a price argument with a customer because that is what a Keeper customer wants. This means slim profits that will in turn drive compromise in product quality. You can see the trap, a low price equals low quality product cycle that will lock a brand out of any chance of becoming a high margin, product-first brand.

The greatest sin might be to believe that "yes" answers to the above questions are any way to run a business. They are not. Certainly not one that is built to be around for the long run. Perhaps there is room for a select few but in a Keeper's world one must know how to be profitable while offering something other than the definitive product – the definitive deal.

Finally, when times get tough, like they did around 2008 and beyond, the Keeper customer will lock up the wallet. Rich Keepers will do the same. In this case, much can be learned by examining the comparative fortunes of GM's luxury brand Cadillac, against the German luxury car brand Audi during the same period.

Taking the year 2007 as a pre-recession year baseline, a two-year drop in sales can be seen at both Audi and Cadillac. The differences, however, are stark. By 2009, Audi had reported a two-year sales drop of 11.5% in U.S. sales. During that same period, Cadillac sales dropped by a stomach-churning 49.2%. Then things really changed. A year later, in 2010, Audi was up by 8.7% from those 2007 numbers while Cadillac sales were still down by 31.6%.

Audi with their sleek European design, excellent handling, and long established and race-proven all-wheel-drive platform (shades of Subaru?) is a car that attracts Finders. The Cadillac, available at all of those GM dealerships across America, is a wealthy and even a high-status Keeper's car. It is also a good example of how when times are tough, they are far tougher for every kind of Keeper-dependent business.

29

◆

THE ELECTRIC CAR-AID ACID TEST

The Chevy Volt

Perhaps we are picking on GM. Ford, Chrysler, and all kinds of other brands and industries in every corner of business have made the same mistakes with policies, marketing strategies, and tactics that would get them the wrong kind of score on that short quiz from a few pages back. Chrysler in particular has spent decades lurching from one near-bankruptcy to another while being passed between various ownership structures like burnt Brussels sprouts at a banquet table.

So it's only fair to give GM a bit of applause. At least for the moment. In the fall of 2010, Chevrolet took a great leap forward with a mix of technology and marketing that could be a game-changer in the automotive industry. The Chevy Volt is an electric powered, plug-in hybrid car that can be driven for hundreds of miles without need of recharge. This affordable electric car could be bought or leased and even purchased at a discount during regular Chevrolet sales events at showrooms across North America. There is much to be said for this car and with sales of over 24,000 in 2013 it is hard to ignore. But was the Volt really the right car in the right place at the right time? Let's look at some numbers. A quick visit to the Chevrolet website will tell you that the 2015 Chevy Volt is priced (as low as!) $26,670. That seems like a bargain. The car has a total range of 58 miles on straight battery and a claimed range of 380 miles while running its small onboard gas generator.

Look at the Volt and you see something that might just transcend Keeper world and become a beloved car for the environmentally conscious Finder looking to spend a few bucks less. After all, it's about the product and not about the money right?

Deduct the rest of North America and you get about 23,000 Volts sold in the U.S. over that network of 4,355 dealerships in 2013; that gives us, on average, 5.3 Chevy Volts sold per dealership. The Malibu is a conventionally powered Chevy with a size and price range that compares well with that of the Volt. During the same period of 2013, 200,954 Malibus were sold through the same dealer network. That comes in at about forty-six per dealership.

Take a new technology, sell it with the assurance of service through America's most abundant dealer network with financing offers and a low price, and one would think that the Volt ought to be the "people's electric car." At just over five per dealership in 2013, it wasn't.

You can't buy a Tesla in Texas

There are a myriad of strange, often dated, and patently unreasonable laws that can be found across various states of the union that prohibit certain car brands from selling their products in certain places. A car dealership is in effect a retailer of a given brand. Tesla eschews that model and sells direct from the factory. This, apparently, is a problem for dealers in a number of states. Otherwise no one would have bothered to lobby so heavily to prevent a direct connection between buyer and builder. Texas is just one of those states; Arizona and New Jersey are two more. Yet, in 2013, while GM was selling those 23,000 Volts at around thirty grand apiece across their big, unfettered dealer network, Tesla sold 18,883 of their electric cars at sixty-one dealerships across North America. Keeping this an apples to apples comparison, that works out to just over 309 Teslas per dealership. If you are keeping score, that is 304 more sales per dealer than the Volt. Tesla dealerships aren't big lots with big signs; they are, for the most part, showrooms located in shopping malls. Finally, the cars sell for about $90,000.

Tesla is an unproven brand, using a new technology that is sold at full retail in sparsely distributed dealerships in only some states in some parts of the country. Compared to the Volt, the Tesla would seem like a dead battery. Except, as the numbers show, it isn't.

The word "dealership" is one that seems to be reserved for the automotive industry. Its etymology of course comes from the word "deal." Whether that particular use of "deal" is in the verb or noun sense is up for debate. Let's change the word dealership for now to what it is in every other retail context: store. If a brand operates a store that is always on sale, it follows that the merchandise available is, at the very least, a compromise in quality, innovation, or any other set of elements that comprise its value. Such a premise runs against the credibility and trust that must be built around any new technology such as the Volt. In this case, a low price simply supports suspicions of compromise.

By being "on sale" at all times, a GM store attracts a customer in search of just that, a sale. A store on sale is a Keeper's environment. Just when General Motors works its way into a leading technological position, it runs up against its most powerful opposition, its own customer.

Keepers are not early technology adopters. This is not news to the car industry. For decades Mercedes has been using its most expensive cars to introduce innovations that, through later economies and wide adoption, have become widespread. Your average Keeper can thank that manufacturer of German luxury lines for everything from the airbag to ABS to the rearview camera on a minivan. That is not to say that only Finders populate the upper income sector where these products are easily adopted; Almost any Finder will adopt relevant technology as soon as he can. If they can't afford a $222,000 AMG S Class Mercedes, you won't see them stealing one for the technology. But you will see them looking for innovation in the cars they can afford. But with all of those cut-price ads and all that brand-speak-before-brand-truth advertising, you won't see many Finders hanging around a General Motors dealership either.

In a move designed to take the Volt's technology up-market, thereby avoiding what the company sees as a late-adopting segment of their customer base, GM has introduced the Cadillac ELR Hybrid. Its performance in the showroom remains to be seen. It is fair to say that in order to attract a technology-loving audience, the company might need to do more than raise a price and offer a car with more features.

Tesla doesn't do dealerships; Tesla does stores. These are cars that are sold on the basis of the company's technological leadership position that has been built on years of research and experimentation and a deep belief, from every corner of that company's culture, in a world that doesn't need fossil fuels. The company is adding further proof to its beliefs by installing a network of charging stations across North America.

You won't ever be encouraged to stop by a monster sale at a Tesla dealership that is sporting a giant inflatable gorilla on its roof. However, you will find the definitive electric car with a sales system and a set of proven values to back it up. Not every Finder has $90,000 to spend on an electric car. Those who have the money and the electric car inclination would make Tesla their first stop. The company's founder and CEO, another strong values-based leader, Elon Musk, has promised that prices will go down as the technology becomes cheaper to produce.

He predicts a $30,000 Tesla in our future. On another note, just by looking at a history littered with the skeletons of "first-in" technologies that can even include what is left of the Blackberry, no one can predict the success or failure of any company that is on the leading edge of any technology. With that disclaimer out of the way, it is safe to say that the fortunes of the electric car or any new technology can be very different depending on which world – Finder or Keeper –that they are for sale in.

30

◆

DUDE, WHERE'S MY CUSTOMER?

Circuit City

If you were in a mood to sum up the end of a business in one sentence, this one might be fitting when it comes to the end of Circuit City: Somebody had to go.

Like Linens N Things, the rise of the category of home electronics came with an equally precipitous fall. If you are old enough to remember a time before the remote control or MTV or, for that matter, HBO, you will recall that a television set was something that sat in the living room of every home in America. It was a fixture with an expected life span to match that of other household appliances. Up until the turn of the millennium, that Sony or Panasonic or even that Zenith or Electrohome TV held a place in the home where it would be expected to stay for about as long as the washer, the fridge, and the hot water tank in the basement. Then along came the flat screen TV. Suddenly every early adopting, TV watching Finder and High Status Keeper was in the market for a TV. A wave hit the electronics business that carried with it ever more technology in the form of surround sound systems and Blu-ray players. New technology had built a profitable and not very price sensitive new consumer willing to pay the big dollar. On the heels of that consumer came bigger electronics retailers and more volume. As technology matured, prices came down and a second wave of customers hit the market in search of the sub $1,000 flat screen TV and under $300 DVD player.

Factories in China, Vietnam, Taiwan, and Korea were built to take full advantage of demand. Soon that one-time $10,000, 32-inch HD TV could be bought for about $700 and everyone could have one. Surround sound packages dropped below $1,000. DVD players fell lower and lower. How was the quality? Look at it this way, for the big home electronics stores, the number one most profitable product sold during the last decade wasn't a product at all, it was the extended warranty. Bargain hunting buyers soon learned, at their peril, that one had best shell out the 10% of purchase price for a warranty or risk a DVD player that began to skip the day after the one year factory warranty dried up.

Then along came Napster. Within a matter of months, the "software" section of every megastore emptied out which meant that the part of the store that generated repeat visits from CD shoppers just didn't anymore. It didn't happen overnight; digital downloading, the Apple Store, and streaming would take a few more years to finish off the CD but the damage was done. The high frequency customers, those who from time to time might drop in for an old Pink Floyd CD and walk out with a new flat screen TV, had become a rarity.

The whole market continued to commoditize. Now that once-coveted flat screen, bought as a better way to watch a good movie by some and bought as a better way to symbolize success by others, could be bought EVERYWHERE. In 2005, you could go to a Best Buy or a Circuit City and pay somewhere around $1,000 for an entry level 32-inch "sort of HD" flat screen. Today you would have a hard time spending $250 on the same size unit while getting far superior performance. Which might be okay until you consider that it can be bought at Costco, Walmart, Target, Big Lots, Kmart, Sears, and, well, everywhere. And then there's online where the buying started with Dell TVs, moved on to Amazon, and then onward to discounters like Newegg and Tiger Direct.

But DVD had a good run. Right? Until video streaming that is. Video streaming, from conventional cable, pirated movies, video subscription streamers – including the granddaddy of them all – Netflix, and online giants Apple Store and Google Play have killed off the DVD. With the death of the DVD comes another empty software section of the store and another product line in the form of DVD players that no one wants anymore.

By 2008, this cycle had finally hit the off switch for Circuit City. Somebody had to go. It might be fair to say that the end may be near for almost everyone else left in the electronics superstore business.

Was this another case of a business caught in that deadly no-man's land between Finders and Keepers? Interestingly, it wasn't. It would be naïve at best, opportunistic at middle, and revisionist at worst to claim that Circuit City would have avoided death by commoditization (Napster and its progeny, streaming video, and competition on all fronts) if it had only sold its goods in some immersive, arty environment filled with unique and definitive products. This wouldn't have and simply couldn't have been the case; Circuit City's problems were just too numerous and unpredictable to have been avoided. There's relevance here that doesn't exist within the story of that retailer's rise and fall; it exists instead in the present and in the future where products that those megastores once thrived on are split into commodities and non-commodities.

31

◆

IT ONLY MATTERS WHEN IT MATTERS

Home Electronics Are Dead. Long Live Home Electronics

Yes there is life after Linens N Things, The Bombay Company, Circuit City, and Detroit bailouts. That form of life can be found just down the logical path from failures in home electronics to wins in the same category.

Finders will behave as Finders when what they are buying matters to them. When it doesn't, they won't. As we saw way back in Chapter 5, when Frank bought himself a cheap TV at Costco, he didn't care much about what he bought so his purchase was based on price. But what if he did care? What if Frank was a dedicated filmophile? (According to the Urban Dictionary this is a real word.) Frank might covet his collection of classic westerns, Japanese sci-fi flicks, and the full set of 1980s John Hughes movies all stored on carefully catalogued VHS, DVD, and Blu-ray. If this were the case you can now imagine him disappearing in a cloud of smoke from that Costco and reappearing in a high end TV specialty store, one that survived the onslaught of those short-lived mega mall electronicosaurs. Frank will have done his research online. He will have kicked the tires on a few models but, in the end, Frank will wind up in the presence of a person who has yet to be mentioned: the Expert.

Throw a dart on a map, land on Omaha, Nebraska, and find the Sound Environment. It's a medium to smallish-sized store staffed with a few different versions of the Expert. There's Charles, who opened the place back when they still called a sound system "Hi-Fi"; and there's Jim, who, with thirty years of home installations experience under his belt, is still something of a rookie at a place that's been in business for forty-five years.

The Omaha version of Frank might be buying a few items at Best Buy, but when it comes to what matters to this movie buff Finder, he'll be looking for plenty of information, he will be in search of products that define quality, and he will just be mad at himself if he makes a compromise based on price. Omaha Frank won't be talking to a so-called expert who has been anointed as such by some noisy advertising campaign; he will be talking to the definitive Expert. And that definitive expert only exists in a specialty store like the Sound Environment.

Here we are then. We have come to the aftermath of a breakdown of the home electronics superstore – not one caused by attention to Finders and Keepers but an industry now broken in half by those two types of consumers. The Sound Environment and its like survived the recession with people who, during that time, kept spending their money. These people were Finders who weren't that fussed by the economic downturn and were still looking for a buying experience that best fit their values. Today, they will carry on with that same kind of buying behavior and those higher-margin, smaller-scale stores like the Sound Environment in Omaha or Acoustic Vision in Missoula, Montana or Reference Media in Bellingham, Washington will remain stable, specialized businesses. Have a look around your town for that home electronics store that survived the supersizing of its category. If it is still there, chances are it will remain there for the long run.

This is Vinyl Tap

The survival of the electronics specialty store as an audiophile or filmophile Finder haven only indicates part of the Finder's relationship with that category. There is in fact a genuine buying phenomenon that is related to the category and it's taking place just down the street; strangely, it is a phenomenon that is taking place in the same category that helped kill Circuit City – software. It is a revival of sorts that is being driven by another kind of Frank – the music freak. This Frank is creating an unprecedented resurgence in what was once the product category that pretty much defined obsolescence: the vinyl record.

The vinyl record and the Finder might be the perfect pairing. You don't really need to be a Finder to understand why. Certainly there are many new vinyl zealots but if you happened to have been a teenage music lover before the emergence and ultimate decline of the CD, you will remember something akin to this testimonial from one of hundreds of thousands of aging vinyl revivalists.

It was September 1977, the month after Elvis died. I got an after-school job as a busboy at a local restaurant. The wage, $3 an hour, plus about $8 to $10 a night in tips. In those days the city's biggest record store, A&B Sound sold LPs starting at $2.99. What a deal! I later learned that this was a "loss-leader" used to attract customers in to buy bigger ticket items among the speakers, receivers, turntables and amplifiers that walled the winding path to the busy checkouts. At $3 an hour I was making one record an hour. Payday came every second Friday. It was on that day that I would get on the bus downtown to A&B Sound for another hit of that high that came in a bright orange bag which when filled, took on that shape that can only be one shape. The shape of a bag of 33 1/3's.

An art director friend once called a record store the ultimate art gallery. He's right. Aisles and walls, rows and bins stuffed with more illustrations, ideas, hair styling, makeup, wardrobe styling, typography and photography than one could ever see in any museum. The time spent in a record store could be hours spent in glorious indecision. Would it be a new release? Would it be something to fill in the back catalogue? Would it be a new sub-genre (art rock, jazz rock, glam rock, prog-rock, folk rock, country rock, new wave, heavy metal, punk, Motown, soul, or (gasp) disco to name a few.) What old band? What new band?

Then there was the trip home, the ceremonial opening of that orange bag, the careful removal of the Mylar cover, the slow reveal of the sleeve, then the record itself and its round stickered center. The liner notes, the lyrics, the credits, the extras like stickers, posters, even in the case of Cheech and Chong's Big Bambu, a giant rolling paper. Then the needle on the record and what might be a week, month or indeed yearlong exploration of each track. Some would change my life. Queen, A Night at The Opera defined tenth grade. Pink Floyd, Dark Side of the Moon convinced all of us, in those long forgotten "drugs are good" years that well, drugs were good. The Clash got us to cut our hair. The Police, Outlandos D'Amour encouraged us to at least consider dying it. Girls, cars, night clubs, sex and travel would follow but as for going shopping, nothing would ever touch that trip to the record store.

What else in the world could offer such immersion? Anyone, Finder or Keeper, who loves music and grew up between the late sixties and the early pre-CD eighties has drunk deep from at least one big cool jug of the Finder life in the form of a shopping trip to buy a fresh batch of vinyl records.

It is no surprise that Finders, with their love of the immersive purchase and everything that goes with it, are driving the highest level of vinyl sales in America in twenty years – up from about 300,000 sold in 2003 to over nine million in 2014. Thanks to the Finder rediscovering his love for the black platter, that starving guy behind the counter in that funky old record store might, for the first time in two decades, be making real money. Is it scalable? Will there be vinyl superstores facing off across shopping mall parking lots in a Finder-enriched future?

Probably not. That nine million number represents 3.6% of all recorded music sales in the U.S. in 2014. The majority of other sales took place the new old-fashioned way, through downloads. Is it sustainable? At around $20 for a record, probably, yes.

Where did all the Keepers Go?

The theme that repeats itself here is that Keepers follow the deal. With few exceptions, big screen TVs are a commodity. (Those exceptions can be found only at opposing poles represented by the extremely high end and costly vs. the shoddily made and laughably cheap.) If such is the case, then you had better find a way to offer the lowest price on the market, period. That is the only way to maintain a relationship with that savvy Keeper.

If you want to know where the Keepers are going, simply look for the retailer or the distribution channel that sells TVs at the lowest price. Increasingly, that channel isn't a store, it's online.

Home electronics are on their way to completing their journey to a true split between Finders and Keepers. Remember that Finders will act like Keepers when there isn't anything about a given product that sets it apart in any way that they care about. To show the split, let's give each side its own definition.

Home Electronics in Keeper World Are: Those that do not offer any definitive, meaningful differences therefore will always be bought on their defining characteristic – the lowest price.

The spoils will always go to he who can offer the lowest price without going out of business.

NOTE: Before we dive in here it is important to observe that this is simply an example of how it works for Finders as it applies to this particular category. In their drive toward getting the real authentic and the definitive, Finders will dig deeply into online sources and secondary information. They will buy from the true experts and will remain loyal to those who align with what is important to them in their search. Remember that they are not simply looking for "the best" as a form of status symbol; they are looking for what will deliver the best performance for their needs.

Home Electronics in a Finders World Are: For Finders who love music or cinema or both, home electronic brands and retailers thrive when the brand produces to a level of proven, demonstrated, and consistent quality that sets it apart from the mass-produced. These brands have a story to tell and will tell that story in an immersive, reasoned, and demonstrable way on a well designed and thoughtfully constructed website that is built to work on desktop and mobile formats. The online story is further supported through engagement in relevant online chat rooms and blogs. You won't find a McIntosh (McIntosh not Macintosh) or a Polk Audio logo plastered on a roadside billboard. Nor will you hear a radio jingle singing its praises. Those brands will only speak quietly through specialized vertical media channels that include audiophile magazines, web advertising on highly relevant sites, and YouTube pre-roll on video content that intersects with Finders' interests. The creative used must not extol brand values unless they directly support the veracity of the product's quality and should seek to demonstrate quality literally or metaphorically but in either case inventively.

Finally, these brands will not be made available at a cost cutter or a megastore; they will instead be for sale (not ON SALE) at a select set of approved retailers who fit the criteria of quality that aligns with the quality of that brand. The product that the brand represents is built to last a lifetime and priced accordingly.

Now comes the store. The retailer will have been in the business for a long time or will at the very least be owned and operated by a seasoned expert and/or preferably a team of experts. These experts share the customer's passion and can completely relate to their needs. It does not help if the retail experts are a bunch of elitist audiophile snobs. Nothing in fact could be worse. This expert must be able to match levels with that Finder customer and be their "connection" in the business, their kind of spirit guide meets Yoda meets electronics nerd. That is the kind of expert who knows how to find out what the Finder wants and gets it to them. And if by any chance he gets it wrong, he is more than happy to correct any issues.

Welcome to Weeper's Home Electronics

Here comes the cautionary tale that, if not heeded, will kick any business back into the weeds. There would be a temptation to try and revive the corpse of Circuit City. Think of all of those vacant stores sitting idle at the end of empty parking lots.

They're depressing. They look like a post-apocalyptic microcosm, a painful and foreboding splinter of what might be. Instead, imagine some bright minded entrepreneur who decides to "get it right" this time. Armed with an optimistic set of spreadsheets, our new retailer calculates revenue on the following basis:

(Average margins of a specialty electronics retailer − 10% competition killing discount on goods) X (projected volume of a volume discounter + diverted customers from specialty stores) or, $(AmSr - 10\%) \times (PvVd + DcSs) = $ Fleet of Private Jets.

What will happen? Likely it will all end in tears. First, should one be lucky enough to secure ANY of those top tier specialty brands, the discounting model will demand compromises in quality of staff (removal of experts), environment, warranty, or after sales service. Going back to those specialty brands, it is highly unlikely that one of those proud manufacturers with their deep connections to the established specialty store would enter into a dalliance with our new store. It is far more likely that the new store will wind up with second-tier brands. To make a long story short, say goodbye to the Finders.

Now we have a store filled with sort-of premium electronics at sort-of-low prices. This is a long way from owning the best deal on what is for most (if the point hasn't been hammered in enough yet) a commodity. You won't even have to say goodbye to the Keepers. They never came in at all.

The moral of this simple cautionary tale is that it is impossible to survive in a world where a business attempts to occupy the middle ground and attract both Finders and Keepers. Choose one or the other. Or go home.

32

◆

FINDERS AT WORK

Up until now we have focused on Finders and Keepers, first through illustrated behaviors and then through their comparative impacts on products and brands. By now the habits and attitudes of the Finder should be quite clear. In this section we will, for the most part, put aside the Keeper and get more specific about how the high consuming Finder can drive success for any number of businesses and organizations though a spectrum of categories.

How on earth can a set of habits found among 46 percent of the population translate into buying power that represents 77 percent of discretionary spending? This leads to a second question, "Where do all these Finders get all this money?" Both are excellent questions.

How do they do it? It all starts with better jobs.

It's 5:00 a.m. in a Los Angeles suburb and if he listens hard enough he can probably hear the REM sleep snores of the neighborhood's still slumbering residents.

Jay is already on his bike. Next weekend he'll be heading

to a stage race in British Columbia's Okanagan Valley and this year he has a bit of a reputation to protect – because last year he actually won a stage. Mid-September temperatures here in L.A. are going to touch the 100s by this afternoon. If he's going to get three hours in on the pedals, he'd best get to it before work.

Right now Jay's job is at Los Angeles based communications, creative and content strategy creation house, Modus Operandi. That's a long description. Modus Operandi connects businesses to customers through everything from YouTube storytelling to mobile applications to interactive games. Jay likes working there on a team where everybody is heading toward the same goals. "There's no negative competition between anyone here. I'm just working with a bunch of incredibly talented people everyday. People who inspire and amaze me." For Jay, this is a stop along a career that has been on a constant upward trajectory for close to twenty years. He's been a brand manager at video game giant, Electronic Arts; he's been an advertising agency art director; he's designed for a snowboard brand – the only job he ever left with the phrase, "Fuck this shit, I quit!" (Interestingly, and completely coincidentally, that was said to then Westbeach Snowboard company owner, Chip Wilson, when Wilson announced that Westbeach would be branching out into rock-climber-inspired fashions. But that is a different story from a long, long pre-yoga-pant time ago). Jay even got fired once for playing practical jokes on customers while an usher at a movie theatre multiplex. He agrees that he basically got fired by getting too bored for his own good. Yes, that was an even longer time ago.

Jay likes to eat at little Mexican joints around town. This, he admits, more than contributed to the sixteen pounds that he's been working off during his race prep. His idea of a great vacation (when he's not spinning pedals on some mountain pass) is to pack a small bag, show up somewhere interesting in the world and, along with his equally adventure-prone wife, feel his way around.

To say that Jay's career has been self-directed would be highly accurate. We could just leave it at that but at the heart of that statement is the "why" of it. To hear him tell it, it sounds like a case of incredible motivation powered by incredible curiosity with perhaps a side of short attention span thrown in. In this way, Jay's career path looks like a squirrel-chasing dog that has figured out how to climb trees. "I was always interested in working on something big so after college I started out by aiming to work at the biggest ad agencies that I could find. I just kept working on my pitch, stayed patient, and corrected course until I got in. Then I just went after producing the best work I could. Then after a while I became fascinated with technology. I researched, then got a job, working in the best place I could find. At the time that was EA (Electronic Arts). After a while, my interests moved toward mobile technology. I wanted to get really good at that, you know, learn it all. So I went after that. That's what I'm doing now." You might have noticed that Jay never waited around and certainly never played politics to move up; he merely worked his ass off at whatever interested him and, when it was time to move on, when he got curious and interested enough, he worked his ass off to get that next, just right job.

"I have never made a single horizontal move in my entire career. I only moved when I could move up." Today, Jay has a highly mobile career, a track record of successes and a broad level of experience in a relatively narrow but seldom-limited field of hiring potential. If he were to check in on former colleagues who have stayed in one place, choosing to patiently climb a ladder, he would happily report another plain fact: Jay makes way better money.

"The reasonable man adapts himself to the world. The unreasonable man adapts the world to himself. All progress depends upon the unreasonable man." ~ George Bernard Shaw.

Here's another question: Who makes more money, a bad employee or a good employee?

A good employee respects authority. He or she helps to keep the company running the way the company is supposed to run. A good employee is loyal, abides by company policies, tows the company line, and interacts well with co-workers. A good employee produces consistent results and can be depended on as a fine representative of the company and, if relevant, its brand. This person is sometimes described as a model employee. This means that he or she stands as a model for job descriptions that might be produced should the need arise to hire additional staff for those particular functions. This in turn makes it easy to take the model employee and replace him or her with a newer model.

A good, agreeable employee will usually earn that description by being just that – agreeable. Which by extension can mean a person who seldom disagrees with superiors and allows, maybe even encourages, those so-called superiors to go forward despite what might be clear errors. An agreeable person seldom challenges convention or steps out of line, never mind stepping on toes. See where this is going?

What we have is a person who can be reproduced, therefore replaced. Replacement often takes place once that good employee begins to earn at a high level for what their job produces. Their job becomes one that can be given to a newer and cheaper employee. Now we have a person who, by not ever disagreeing with managers or clients, does not push boundaries or prevent myopic, Titanic-into-iceberg collisions. A good employee is just that, good, not great. A good employee can make good money but, more often than not, a good employee makes only good money, never great.

A bad employee gets fired. Fired for insubordination, fired for taking unreasonable risks, fired for telling a dickhead client what kind of a dickhead he is. A bad employee gets fired for being terrible at a job that she's just not cut out for. Then a bad employee gets a better job and probably gets fired again. Or a bad employee is loyal not to the company but him- or herself and doesn't need to get fired. That bad employee quits and keeps quitting until the best job is found.

A bad employee is an employee who winds up as an entrepreneur, or as a valued, risk-taking innovator, or a high-producing salesperson with that big personality and creative approach. A bad employee either makes it or breaks it. And if he or she breaks it, a lesson is learned, a course is corrected, and the journey onward continues.

Advertising creative legend and alleged pain-in-the-ass, Paul Arden, supports this thinking in his aptly named book, *Whatever You Think, Think the Opposite*. The whole book is only about 2,000 words long and reads like a rant from a successfully bad employee. Chapters come with titles such as, "The Case for Being Reckless;" "Do It and Fix It as You Go;" and "It Is Better to Regret What You Have Done Than What You Haven't."

It is all highly inspirational stuff but Arden would surely agree that this "good employee, bad employee" distinction is, without some other very important ingredients like hard work, smarts, and opportunity, just a fluffy, aphorism filled speech. Being a bad employee is just a part of the Finder career story and reveals a fundamental difference between career attitudes in Finders and Keepers.

A Keeper will often view herself as an employee who works for someone else. A Finder on the other hand will almost always look on herself, even if employed in exactly the same job as that Keeper, as working for herself and as such, responsible for her own path. Or in Jay's case his path.

It is in their careers where Finders reach the intersection

between their values and success. A lack of respect for convention is one thing, but it is the need to discover and a love of the new that drives them to work obsessively at the things that they are most attracted to.

"Working really hard is what successful people do..."
~ Malcolm Gladwell, *Outliers: The Story of Success.*

Malcolm Gladwell's 2008 book *Outliers: The Story of Success* could be considered the gold standard in studies on success. It considers and weighs the combinations of connections, innate talent, societal constructs, and even birth month. His exhaustively researched book most certainly examines personality traits that include a healthy disrespect for authority, but Gladwell makes it clear that it would be foolish to try to shoehorn all of the success factors listed here into the consumer profile of a Finder. Its real relevance comes to light when considering Gladwell's most consistent success factor: hard work.

If you are a donkey, there are two kinds of motivations: the carrot and the stick. More often than not, carrot and stick are looked at as the two poles of motivation. The stick is perhaps the worst motivator invented. One can only work so hard when motivated by fear, intimidation, or thoughts of a proverbial wolf at the door. The carrot, the idea of financial reward for the sake of the reward itself, does not often create long-term job satisfaction in itself either. Certainly the idea of a nicer car or a bigger boat can drive some forward in the most soul crushing of jobs but this doesn't often work to bring consistent thought, dedication, and imagination to long hours and hard challenges. For Finders, neither carrot nor stick applies. For Finders, it is the job itself.

"Work freely and rollickingly as though you were talking to a friend who loves you. Mentally (at least three or four times a day) thumb your nose at all know-it-alls, jeerers, critics, doubters." ~ Brenda Ueland, *If You Want to Write: A Book About Art, Independence and Spirit.*

There is a formula for success among Finders and it can be found when key Finder characteristics are applied to other markers of career advancement and their attendant financial rewards. These six key characteristics bear repeating:

Finders are masters of their own universe. Finders are individualists who believe that they make their own way in the world with their own talents, skills, and planning. They believe far more in self-determination than following tradition and authority.

Finders love the story. Where it came from, what it's about, how it's made, who made it or created it; the provenance of the product is key. Finders have a huge appetite for real and rich information, not hyperbole. They will read more and look for more. The more they know, the more value a product has to them.

Finders find. Finders will try something new first. Not to simply be first as a symbol of status but to have the adventure of discovery in the new and the sense of individuality that comes with <u>being a pioneer</u> in adopting something new.

Finders are leading edge. Finders are always the <u>first to adopt new technologies</u> and remain the heaviest users of the Internet. They are reluctant to accept any second-bests when it comes to technology.

Finders are elastic in their careers. A strong appetite for learning and personal development, the search for the new, and a hunger for information are traits that transcend mere consumption among Finders and drive them toward increased <u>mobility and exploration</u> in their careers. Individualism and less of an adherence to playing by conventional rules means a strong entrepreneurial streak among Finders.

Now, let us take all of those underlined words shown above and describe a person: A Finder is an <u>individualist</u> with <u>a huge appetite for real and rich information</u>, a <u>pioneer, first to adopt new technologies,</u> and she approaches her career with <u>mobility and exploration</u>.

What we have in a Finder at work is a person who seeks out the job that best fits, applies herself to it with love and hard work, and creates results as a byproduct of that love.

Finders include that man with the $54 million waterfront home built from a definitive yoga pant, or the empire-building espresso aficionado with a net worth of $2.3 billion. But they are also the ones that you'll bump into at the taco bar, guys like Jay who couldn't walk away from an obsession with creating his own best in class and gave himself permission and flexibility to travel in the direction of his passions.

33

ARE YOU GONNA EAT THAT? FINDERS AND DINING

"Our menu is meant for sharing, just order one dish at a time, we'll put it in the middle of the table and you guys can go to it. If you like, I'll suggest a few wines, cocktails, or craft beers to go with anything you order." She makes a few suggestions, recounts a short anecdote about a certain cocktail, gets the first of what will be eight different orders from that one table, and dashes off in a thrift store clad, tattooed blur. A cooking line breathes fire from just behind a row of low shelves stocked with the day's fresh produce and local organics. A bar hewn from recycled timber runs below high library shelves stocked with micro-spirits to create a wall of wood and alcohol that anchors the raw concrete north end of the room. Wine seems to be stored in every available nook and cranny of this stripped out old storefront. The menu is a simple two-sided affair that explores the nearby waters of the Oregon Coast, the farmland and vineyards of the Columbia River Gorge, and the breweries and micro-distilleries of the once-abandoned industrial heaps that flank the city's riverbanks. It's 9:30 Sunday night in downtown Portland as another menu exploration begins at Tasty N Alder. Welcome to what might be the bull's eye in America's newest culinary epicenter. Humming, banging, and blazing along, full to the sidewalk on a school night serving what is way beyond fine without ever being fine dining, Tasty N Alder is casual in hospitality and fiercely professional in product. One does not need to dress up to go there.

It is a one-off restaurant that packs in diners who are in search of great food and a real, authentic, and original dining experience. There are thousands of its kind proliferating across America – each with its own name, identity, owners, menu, sources, décor, ethics, and idiosyncrasies. Not one of them can be accused of being a "brand." Each is simply as good a product as that particular set of servers, bartenders, chefs, and creators can come up with. They live and die on their own merits and any kind of compromise will end in quite certain bankruptcy.

Meanwhile, in the malls and down the off ramps of this very same country there is another kind of casual dining. In this case the servers wear uniforms and the menu is worded in friendly, unthreatening "brand-language." This is a Chili's, an Olive Garden, an Outback Steakhouse, a Cheesecake Factory, a Sizzler, or a TGI Fridays. These are brands that define what industry analysts call Casual Dining. These are trustworthy names that specialize in meeting expectations. On a Saturday night when a couple wants to get a sitter and go out, any one can be a reliable place that sits firmly in a comfort zone of expectation around its food, service, décor, dress code, and price. We'll go one further than calling it Casual Dining – we'll call this Branded Casual Dining.

Restaurant usage habits draw a clear border between Finder and Keeper. Sunday night in Portland, Tasty N Alder is packed with Finders. Down the I-5 on the way to the university town of Eugene, there's a Chili's. Business is a little slow on Sunday night at 9:30. Saturday night was a little better. Chili's advertises free chips and queso with its dinners. Maybe that is a response to the all-you-can-eat breadsticks at the nearby Olive Garden. Chili's and its kind aren't located that far from Tasty N Alder but they live in a totally different world, the Keeper's world.

Maybe the web ads trumpeting 2 for1 Fajitas at Chili's are a dead giveaway but price doesn't really tell the story. It is in fact a mistake to think of the divide between the Finder and Keeper restaurant as one drawn out by a line of dollar bills. For example, a Kobe steak and frites (fries) at Tasty N Alder is an even $17. A middle of the price range sirloin steak at Chili's is just seventy-one cents cheaper at a Walmart-esque $16.29. The divisions between Finders and Keepers in dining might be defined, to a certain degree, by at least a perceived price division. Yet to simply divide dining by dollars misses the point. This is where we return to another currency with another exchange rate between Finder and Keeper worlds. The currency of time.

To a Keeper, time is to be spent carefully. By getting that sitter, the Keeper has already paid real money for time, but take the sitter, or any other cost out of the equation, and there still exists a need to get a guaranteed return on time. An established, branded food experience with an expected, hit-it-down-the-middle menu of comfortable choices means a guaranteed return – not necessarily a high return – on the expenditure of that Saturday night. Only after the currency of time is taken into consideration can you turn your attention to those all-you-can-eat, free bonus values that hit the dollar-aroused Keeper pleasure centers.

By looking at all those brands and all of those locations, one might assume the branded casual dining concepts to be a Keeper-driven winner. Before we do, let us remember that Keepers only account for a fraction of disposable expenditures. Disposable expenditures are exactly what pay the bills for the restaurant industry, which means that with price competition there will always be a brick wall at the end of the Keeper expansion road. So what does happen when you make food about brand and price? Bad things happen.

Bad things like this. Today it looks as though the branded casual dining segment might have had an extra helping of post-sell-by-date signature dipping sauce. By 2012, business at the Country Kitchen chain was puking its guts out with an 82% drop in trade. In that same year, over half of all Ponderosa and Bonanza Steak Houses in America, ("Where today's families find the spirit of the Old West, the flavors they crave, and something-for-everyone variety") had slammed their collective barn doors for good. In 2013, Forbes Magazine reported that long time industry leaders Red Lobster, Olive Garden, and Longhorn Steakhouse had been in negative growth since 2012.

These are tough times for the restaurants of Keepers' world.

It's the opposite at the Finder's table. An altogether different tale from that of the Keeper feeders can be told at the lunch counters, breakfast joints, and Finder-attractive places of every flavor including (gasp) fast food. Let's dig in shall we?

It might be a chicken and egg sort of question when one asks, "Do Finders have more discerning palates than Keepers?" The simple answer could be yes. That yes has most likely developed out of other Finder habits. One cannot live by a quest for real authenticity in life, an exploratory spirit, or a love of the aesthetic without coming up against food. By seeking these qualities in food, Finders develop habits that are just that, repeated behaviors. If you have ever bought a Farmer's market tomato freshly picked during the height of the season and eaten it like a very juicy plumb, you will know that there is a huge difference PLUM between that tomato and its distant mid-winter supermarket step-cousin. Once you have had that sort of tomato epiphany your definition is changed for good. If on the other hand you have only enjoyed the mealy, watery, ripened-on-the-shelf version, well, that is what a tomato is to you. Simple.

Food then might come down to a question of taste but any given consumer's idea of what constitutes that taste comes down to experience. And experience takes exploration.

Exploration is the territory of the Finder. The Finder

looks at a great meal as something filled with examples, like that market tomato, from a universe of back-story, and flavors. A Keeper looks at dining out in different terms including predictability, assurance, and value. The food is a mix of flavors that he knows he likes and the value is expressed by portion size and price. The assurance is built out of a brand and out of familiarity.

So why is one kind of restaurant category growing while the other fails? Finders and Keepers just don't change sides. It is not that there are more Finders being made out of ex-Keepers, that's not going to happen. Instead, this is a case of existing demand falling in love with a new supply. As more chefs and restaurateurs create mixes of foods and environments that fit the Finder diner, Finders gain new choices that go way beyond what they never much liked in the first place. They just don't have to go to the Cheesecake Factory anymore.

Interestingly, a lot of this has to do with a post-recession world. Back in Portland that night at Tasty N Alder wasn't brought to you by a stand-alone, purpose-built building with plenty of parking; it was instead discovered in yet another retail space that had been decimated by the recession. In a cyclic turnaround from that recession, the devaluation of real estate has worked to create accidental economic zones where independents can now afford to ply their art – at the perhaps expense of 2 for 1 Fajita Night at Chili's.

They don't call it the culinary arts for nothing and there is in fact a strong connection between the food and the art world here. As far as artists go, there is a trend toward more artists per capita living and creating in cheap old warehouse spaces in rust belt cities like Pittsburg than high rent lofts in New York's Soho. In Europe, euro gobbling Paris is far less of a petri dish for new art than cheap-rent and squatter-tolerating Berlin. So goes the same trend with food in the still mostly-dead zones of many of the post-recession downtowns of America. It is here that a new kind of dining scene is rising like a perfectly braised free-range Phoenix from the storefront ashes of the early millennium.

There we have it, a new culinary level of creativity finds a ready, willing, and paying customer in a Finder who has always felt uncomfortable eating a brand instead of a meal, in a match made in cheap real estate heaven.

34

◆

THE FAST AND THE EPICURIOUS

Finders at the Drive-Thru

Having established a Finder-driven move away from that meal that comes bearing the name of a chain, there is still much to be learned in a new form of branded dining – one that brings in the Finder. There may be few reasons to believe that anyone is going to unseat McDonald's from its dominant place in the drive-thru world of fast food America but that world itself is changing. Over the last decade or so, the golden arches grew by around 2% per year. With a size and market penetration that sits way beyond its nearest competitor, that 2% represented a healthy growth trend. Then the good news at Mickey D's got a bit soggy. By 2014, growth had reversed to show a drop in sales of 2.9%. By the third quarter of 2014, that drop had accelerated to 3.3%. There is evidence that this sudden downturn might grow into a long-term trend. McDonald's, as a flagship Keeper brand, is suffering from the same price and cost pressures that exist across the Keeper spectrum. In October 2014, Bloomberg Business reported that the chain had been forced to apply a price increase during that year to cover rising wage costs and commodity prices. This led to a loss of price-sensitive customers who left in search of a better deal. They might have found it at Burger King where a ten pack of chicken nuggets was featured at $1.49. Even for McDonald's, a lead that is held by a lowest price can only ever be temporary.

McDonald's is responding with renovated restaurants, mobile ordering and payments, and, in a somewhat accidentally Finder-ish way, installing burger customizing and ordering touch-screens in some of its restaurants.

Old Ronald McDonald is not the interesting story here. He's just setting the stage. Over the past five years the fast casual chain, Chipotle Mexican Grill, has seen steady, year-on-year revenue growth of 20% per year.

One might expect a lot of slogans from a fast food joint; Chipotle's "Food With Integrity" might not be one of them. In a multi-award winning web ad titled "The Scarecrow," the brand tells a redemptive story that begins in a dark and terrifying world of factory farming set to a bleak rendition of the Willy Wonka movie song, "Pure Imagination." The year before that, Chipotle told much the same tale to Willy Nelson singing Coldplay's "Back to the Start." Each garnered tens of millions of YouTube views. These commercials did not include any artistically filmed flying food. There were no grinning and chewing kids; there was just a heart-first story about how factory-farmed food might not be the best way to live.

Need any proof as to whether Finders have embraced Chipotle as their go-to fast food? It might be best told in a May 2014 article on Slate.com titled, "Why Chipotle Customers Don't Care About Rising Burrito Costs."

The article reports on Chipotle's need to respond to rising commodity prices by passing those costs on to customers. Within the article stands this quote from Morningstar's senior restaurant analyst, R.J. Hottovy:

"...Hottovy...outlines three other things that work in Chipotle's favor over other fast-food and fast-casual restaurants: (1) the food quality is thought to be higher; (2) the service is generally better; and (3) the customers that eat there tend to be more affluent. "With strong customer loyalty scores and a perception of higher-quality ingredients, we believe the Chipotle brand possesses more pricing power than other restaurant peers, as evidenced by an average check of more than $10 per customer and menu price increases in each of the last five years."

By getting its values out on its sleeve and sticking to its product while trusting its customers to participate in what a fair price needs to be, Chipotle has achieved that impressive and rare feat: it has built a Finder brand and then made it scalable.

Chipotle gets categorized within its industry under a few titles: Premium Quick Service Restaurant (PQSR) or Fast Casual. These descriptions tend to mislead. Look at the description of Premium Quick Service Restaurant. If one were to simply open a more expensive burger joint with expectations of runaway growth between a thicker patty and a better bun then failure can be expected.

However, it can be done. Five Guys Burger and Fries does a great job of making a burger that a small but pretty committed slice of the population would call the definitive burger. It even comes with a good backstory.

Otherwise there is nothing to be gained by simply taking an extremely widespread concept and making it a little bigger and a little more expensive. The assumption that a QSR will do better if its initials start with the P for Premium is one that will more likely drive a business concept into something that lands between QSR and nothing at all. Chipotle competes with innumerable burrito joints and again it would be a mistake to distill its success into a claim, real or perceived, that it makes the best burrito in the world. It probably doesn't. Chipotle has built a scalable Finder brand by underpinning the quality of what that brand delivers in another way. It has done it by standing by its ethics. That does sound like a weird concept when speaking of fast food, but that is what it is. In this way, Chipotle equals a great burrito not because it has been "branded" to mean Chipotle = Best Burrito; instead it makes a more meaningful point by being less explicit and letting the customer figure the product out for herself. In her mind Chipotle equals Trust. Trust, in this case, means a strong self-identification with a brand that will always do the right thing. So Chipotle has a strong ethic around farming and food supply. By proving that it can be trusted to follow through on that particular ethic, the brand earns trust that translates into something that is more relevant at the store level. That is, if Chipotle stands by what it says, and it also says it makes a great burrito, well, then it makes a great burrito. Or bowl. Or salad.

These ethics need to be relevant and it helps that they speak to food quality. They should. If Chipotle were to build its ethics around say, saving mountain gorillas, then the brand would still be engaged in a noble cause but it would have trouble building cause into the story of its food.

Price only enters into one part of the Chipotle story and it's a good one. By simply existing in a premium but not insanely expensive price bracket, Chipotle gets the whole enchilada: Finders and Evolving Finders.

Is Chipotle the perfect Finder brand then? It certainly wins on the quality and authenticity scales with real ingredients that are uncommon in a quick service restaurant. That is as far as the authentic claim can go. Chipotle is many things but it does not truly connect with the culture of its foods' origins. If it did, it would serve truly authentic Mexican food made by Mexican chefs using authentic recipes. In a recent Instagram post one wiseass and presumably Hispanic person commented on a Chipotle advertisement for a pumpkin themed Thanksgiving burrito with the comment, "This is what happens when white people try to make our food." Origins aside, Chipotle has strong values, makes food that isn't full of crap, and sticks to its product without ever blinking in the face of compromise. It might not be the authentic fish taco from Ensenada, but it is most certainly true to its promise of quality.

Chipotle invites both kinds of Finders to its lineups but do Evolving Finders have their own thing? To watch the proliferation of Food Trucks across the nation is to get the answer. Come lunchtime in any city, a natural sortation process between Finder and Keeper gets played out as lunch breakers split off between Burger King and Subway storefronts and those Taco, Korean BBQ, Northern Indian, Grilled Cheese, Poutine, Raw Juice, and Mac and Cheese Trucks that just keep mutating and dividing all over the urban streets.

A full house on a Sunday night at a one-off restaurant in Portland, lineups at Chipotle, and convoys of food trucks do not tell the entire tale. Instead, smaller trends might do well to illustrate the larger scene and its long term potential. This brings us to that seed crop of emerging Finders, the often millennial Evolving Finders. It is hard to imagine that the future will hold much room for ever-growing chains of restaurants that serve pretty much the same fare in a world where cities are beginning to create a subculture of young, highly sophisticated diners who choose dining out, and dining out well, over moving out of their parent's basements. That subculture exists and is growing.

In an October 2012 article in Britain's *The Telegraph* titled, "The gastronauts: London's new breed of restaurant-goer," Lucy Cavendish called dining "the new rock and roll" where almost every night of the week the junior salary millennial crowd strikes out in search of the sharpest edge of the wedge in dining. The trend that began in New York a few years back has spread to cities all over the globe where the expansive culinary scene's only real constant is change. These London versions of the gastronaut will spend up to £300 per week (about $490) on their kind of finely tuned dining. This means that they will often give up an outsized portion of their salaries to their palates in exchange for almost anything (the kind of anything that more often than not means a much lengthened occupancy of a childhood bedroom under a parent's roof). Like rock and roll in its once dangerous early days, tucking into rosehip infused quail in lieu of more common societal norms might seem like mildly anti-social behavior but it paints a picture. In this case one that shows the willingness among a less moneyed Finder subset to compromise something expected in the search for something new. Gastronauts might seem like an insane form of indulgence to some but for these millenial Evolving Finders it's just another kind of exploration.

35

THERE IS NO SUCH THING AS FREE RANGE CONCRETE: FINDERS AND REAL ESTATE

Four Seasons Private Residences Denver - A Case Study

Author's Note: Hello reader, I hope you have enjoyed the book so far. I am stepping out of the narration for a moment to set you up for this chapter. Much of the inspiration for this book is from the gentleman that we'll be talking about here, Chris Norton. His own book written with Ross Honeywill in 2012, *One Hundred Thirteen Million Markets of One*, and Honeywill's breakthrough research and resulting book, *NEO Power*, have been key source material for *Finders & Keepers*. While you might have been reading my words, I have often felt Chris at my shoulder during the writing process. Norton and Honeywill's original definition of Finders is NEOs (New Economic Order). In the case of Keepers, Norton and Honeywill call them Traditionals. Both definitions will be used in this chapter while we tell the story of Four Seasons Private Residences Denver. On another note, it bears mentioning that I am Creative Director and a partner at Spring Advertising. With partners Richard Bergin and James Filbry, and our screamingly talented team, we conceived and produced the advertising campaign on the project covered in this chapter. Please, forgive the intrusion and read on.

It is 3:00 p.m. on yet another sunny May afternoon in Colorado's mile high city. Chris Norton is walking the perfectly finished hardwood floor of a 3,500 square feet apartment some thirty floors up in the Four Seasons Private Residences Denver. The view from this lofty and pricy overlook is quite spectacular. It includes mountains, the full complement of Denver's many sports stadiums and arenas, and – if one could see with the finest detail through trees, buildings, overpasses and neighborhood hedges – a very large number of "FOR SALE" signs and foreclosure placards. It is 2010 and property values in Denver, like the rest of the country, are so far in the tank, they're under it.

Yet here is Chris, a somewhat reluctant real estate marketing specialist, on his way to selling another multi-million dollar condominium at full price carrying with it a near $100,000 annual strata fee.

Before you make any assumptions about the so-called one percent, take this into consideration. Until Mr. Norton came to town, not one single home priced at over $1,000,000 had sold in the Greater Denver Area since 2007. Apart from the Four Seasons Private Residences Denver, they still weren't selling.

Chris doesn't see himself as a real estate marketer or agent. In fact, if you were to call him that to his face, you might hurt his feelings. Chris is one of the world's pre-eminent authorities on the NEO typology, those behavioral factors that describe the very people that this book defines as Finders. Today he is selling real estate; next, he will be consulting to a gigantic food brand, then a network of furniture retailers, and then a drug store chain. After that, he might just change the world. Keep an eye out for his latest venture, Crowdspending. It is his genius solution for un-commoditizing the commoditized, and empowering people everywhere to change the world with their own personal and specific values.

On this day in 2010, Chris' company, Fingerprint Solutions, has been tasked with selling the unsellable: 110 luxury "private residence" condominiums perched on the top twenty-two floors of Denver's spanking new Four Seasons Hotel.

If one were to build some kind of depressing monument to the real estate crash that took place during the last years of this century's first decade, that monument might come in the form of an idle and rusting construction crane. There was a time, not so long ago, when almost every city in America had their own example, or in many cases, dozens of examples of abandoned cranes sitting mournfully atop the open concrete and rusting rebar of an unfinished hotel – one that was to have been funded in part by luxury condominiums. This idea was conceived during the boom bubble days, around 2005. When the bubble went pop in 2008, sales of those lifestyle palaces in the sky dove right off the top of those suddenly idle cranes.

What was the natural reaction among Keeper thinking developers? Act on the assumption that High Income/High Status Keepers, what Norton calls High Status Traditionals, would respond to the deal and drop prices. This of course only made things worse as those with the money put away their wallets and began to play the game of "Watch the Price Drop."

Chris Norton illustrates the price drop game among the wealthy Traditionals with this story from his book, *One Hundred Thirteen Million Markets of One.*

"One High Status Traditional client of ours, who is very wealthy and enjoys a fabulous lifestyle of private planes, luxury homes and fast cars stayed recently at a major hotel in Las Vegas. He knew they had condos for sale and that the market there was awful, so he asked the brokers how much for the penthouse. Quoted a list price of $12 Million, he pulled out his checkbook and handed them a check for $1 Million saying, 'I'm leaving on Monday, let me know if you are going to cash it.'"

This kind of high-rolling waiting game was just another problem that was further compounded by a whole set of other issues. First, a lack of credit meant a lack of sales for any property thereby knocking out any consumer who needed to sell a property before taking on the luxury hotel condominium lifestyle. For any developer building a Ritz Carlton Hotel with a Private Residence on top, or a similar Shangri-La, W Hotels, or Four Seasons, times were tough. Sell the yacht and fly economy tough.

While those two stakes were being driven into the heart of the luxury condominium market, another reality showed up to throw a bucket of gas on it and light a match: return on investment. Boom times always create real estate investment markets – an obvious point but worth mentioning. After a few decades of quite steady growth in the U.S. real estate market, homeowners stopped looking at the old homestead as a residence and began to look at it as an investment that would be expected to generate a return. Then, by just adding a line of credit or a second mortgage, any homeowner – from entry-level condo buyer to penthouse owning plutocrat – could turn home sweet home into home sweet bank account.

The Assignment: Sell the bulk of 110 luxury condominiums ranging in price from $2,000,000 to $10,000,000 before the bank pulls financing and the whole project goes bust.

This is what Norton and his team were up against in 2010. To put it in marketing terms, the situation analysis on the briefing document could be summed up in two words, "We're fucked."

One would certainly have every reason to think so. Yet by the end of 2012, Four Seasons Private Residences Denver was sold out. A full year ahead of the projected and highly unrealistic schedule set by its new owner. The first owners of course had already gone out of business leaving a few private jet loads of airsick lenders in their wake.

What happened? Chris, his sales team, and his advertising agency, Spring, came up with a strategy that traveled in the opposite direction of convention with a set of "what ifs?" They went something like this:

1. What if we worked on the premise that Four Seasons Private Residences Denver (FSPRD) was a lousy financial investment but worth buying anyway? After all, nobody buys a boat as an investment. Why not let the fact that this is not a financial investment just hang right out there?

2. What if we looked at FSPRD as a NEO (Finder) product? Four Seasons, with its incredibly strong values around service, its *definitive* level of service (for residents in particular), and its ability to create a bespoke lifestyle environment for owners gives it at least the potential to be a NEO product. In real estate, would it be possible to turn the tables and go for a product-before-price customer proposition?

3. What if we create a customer proposition that spoke to the concept of a life lived on one's own terms with absolutely no complications or unwanted inconveniences, all made possible by Four Seasons services and amenities?

4. What if we re-engineered the pricing to create a pricing structure that would sell prime units to NEOs at no discount, but would make less appealing units available at slightly lower prices to attract High Status Traditionals who were after the status afforded by the Four Seasons brand but stimulated into buying only by a

discount. (The building has some spectacular views and boasts some quite impressive architecture in most of its residences but, being a four sided structure in a city that even proud Denver residents might admit contains a few ugly buildings, Four Seasons Private Residences has a few less than jaw dropping views in a few awkwardly designed spaces.) This sub-strategy had an interesting effect in itself. Once full-priced units began to sell in the building, they set up a pricing benchmark that was no longer based on real estate pricing comparables from around the market (which were in the toilet) but instead depended on pricing within the building itself. That meant that a discount for a wealthy High Status Traditional (Keeper) wasn't a desperate price cut as seen in every other similar market in the country, it was a modest reduction from the full price within Four Seasons Private Residences Denver itself.

To this last point you might be saying, "Wait! You said that you can't sell to Finders and Keepers at the same time!" You would be correct. In the case of FSPRD the product was split into two different products. One: home as the ultimate in personalized lifestyle enabling, and two: a status brand at a discount. That sort of distinction is extremely rare in the two worlds of Finders and Keepers but was achieved in this case.

All of these hypotheses were put to the test. It started with an almost five minute long online film that might have broken records for production costs among real estate advertising. One thing is for certain. It united the lenders and Four Seasons Corporate Office in one thing, they all hated it.

THIS IS YOUR TIME

EXT: MOUNTAIN RUNNING TRAIL — PRESENT DAY — EARLY
     MORNING

A MAN in his late 40s is running a well-worn path up a hill through trees and brush. As he runs we CUT back and forth from his run to his thoughts of his life.

Flashback to:

EXT: CAR INTERIOR — 1968

Man, now a BOY of seven rides in the back of a 1965 Ford Station Wagon with his OLDER SISTER behind him, his parents in the front as DAD drives. Dad is turning angrily to the boy to answer a question to what can be seen as, "what time is it?"

                    DAD

Five minutes after the last time you asked!

EXT: SCHOOL — 1969

It is the first day of school and first day of first grade for Boy. A banner reads "WELCOME BACK

STUDENTS!" Children run down the steps of school,
Boy and his FRIEND exit behind the crowd. Boy looks
shocked and appalled.

> BOY
> (incredulous)
> Twelve more years?!?!

INT: FAMILY HOME, DINING ROOM — 1970

Boy is seated at the head of the table with a 10th
birthday cake in view. Dad, with cigarette in one
hand and drink in the other, has been berating the
family. He stops to change the mood by producing
a gift from his shirt pocket for the boy. It is
a watch. The boy is delighted until his father
reaches across the table and drops the watch into
the Boy's full water glass.

EXT: FAMILY HOME SWIMMING POOL — LATER

We are underwater in the family's small swimming
pool. The Boy appears to be floating beneath the
surface. The still body suddenly comes to life as
the boy swims to the surface looking at his watch.
We can now see that Dad's water glass treatment was
just a demonstration of the waterproof watch.

EXT: MOUNTAIN RUNNING TRAIL — PRESENT DAY — EARLY
     MORNING

We cut back to the solitary runner and flashback to…

INT: FAMILY HOME KITCHEN — 1970

It is the last day of the school year as Boy runs
in from the back door with his bag of books as Mom
looks on, he's elated.

                    BOY
        3 months! That's like forever!

INT: FAMILY HOME KITCHEN — 1977

We cut seven years into the future, Boy is now
Teenage Boy. He is completely depressed at the
prospect of school at the end of summer. We cut in
such a way to allow him to appear almost as if he
is arguing with his younger, early summer self.

                TEENAGE BOY
        3 months! Not enough time!

INT: FAMILY HOME KITCHEN — VERY LATE NIGHT

An engine can be heard approaching in the distance.
The kitchen clock reads 3:45. CUT TO:

EXT: FAMILY HOME DRIVEWAY — VERY LATE NIGHT - 1977

An old beater car pulls up on the street above the
home's sloping driveway, the engine shuts off and
the lights go out. A late 50s Corvette is parked at
the bottom of the driveway. Teenage Boy is sneaking

home late, he shuts off the car and rolls to the
edge of the driveway and gets out to quietly push
from the open driver side door to ease it over the
slight curb on the transition between road and
driveway. He trips at the curb and the car gets
away from him, rolling down the driveway and into
the Corvette with an earsplitting crash.

EXT: MOUNTAIN RUNNING TRAIL — 1977 — EARLY MORNING

A slightly paunchy Teenage Boy in jean shorts and
sneakers struggles to jog up the running trail
for what is his first of countless runs on it. He
struggles to the apex and, almost vomiting, checks
his watch, the same one that Dad had given him
years before.

EXT: MOUNTAIN RUNNING TRAIL — 1987 — EARLY MORNING

Teenage Boy is now an athletic Young Man. As he runs
a YOUNG WOMAN passes near the summit. He quickens
pace and reaches the top just behind her. He can't
break what is now the habit of checking his watch
but is distracted by her beauty. He glances up from
the watch and the two lock eyes.

                    YOUNG MAN
                    Fast!

She smiles and laughs.

242 FINDERS & KEEPERS

This is what they call in the screenwriting business a "meet cute." A rocky romance begins between the two and we follow our Man as he goes through starting a business to losing his father to losing his girl to getting her back again thanks to a collision between his bike and her car, to getting married, to having a child, to that child growing to adulthood and moving out. Throughout the film the only dialogue is spoken in measures of time like "too soon" and "already" and "not another minute." Let's jump to the end now.

EXT: MOUNTAIN RUNNING TRAIL — PRESENT DAY — EARLY
    MORNING

Finally, we find our hero, now in middle age as he once again reaches the top of his hill. He is alone for a moment, but then our girl, now his long time wife, runs up behind him.

WIFE
What time is it?

Man glances at his now old and trusted watch. We come in close to see that it has stopped. He shakes it a few times and a thought strikes him. He gazes into the middle distance for a moment then turns to his wife.

MAN
Now.

She takes this in and smiles knowingly.

FADE TO: BLACK TITLE CARD

Reads: This is Your Time.
        Four Seasons Private Residences Denver.

No smiling doormen, no massage tables, no camera filtered views, no sexy canoodling couple at the bar, and no slow-motion flames from a shrimp flambé while it dances in its pan atop the high-end gas range. Instead, a bit of a tearjerker about how time can rule us, and a message that lets the audience reach a conclusion. That conclusion could be best described as, "You've spent your whole life being chased around by time, you've earned the right to take control of it. And Four Seasons Private Residences Denver is the way to do so."

They hated it. Which was perfectly fine because "they" weren't the audience. Wealthy time-exhausted Finders with sensitive, creative spirits, and functioning tear ducts were. The film was promoted using rich media web banner ads in a form that approximated extremely short movie trailers. The banner ads invited viewers to watch the movie. Nothing more.

By matching online media outlets with an algorithm developed using NEO typology variables – the same data that parts of this book are based on – Spring's media buyers were able to isolate Finder user groups, plan and buy media, and quickly correct course based on comparative click-through rate performances.

When users clicked through to the website they were treated to a full version of the film and then introduced to a website that customized the user experience according to the user's hopes, dreams, and ambitions. It worked by asking users questions about where that user would like to be in life over the next six months, two years, and five years. This was done with a series of multiple-choice questions. Then, once the answers had been provided, the site offered up a personalized film of what that person's life might look like if they lived a Four Seasons Private Residences Denver life. This was achieved through a point of view (POV) video cut using a real-time editing algorithm that drew from a large library of pre-shot POV camera footage of a person engaging in a wide variety of activities. This way, if a user was to respond to questions with answers such as, "Live a fit, energetic life, spend more time with my family, travel more, and never cook again" she would be served a video that showed a personal trainer picking her up at the door and taking her through a training session, children coming to visit and playing in the pool, a bellman loading luggage into a car, and a doorman welcoming her (or them) at another Four Seasons and, finally, a catered, in-suite meal. These personal mini-films were easily shareable and led to the more functional parts of the site, one of which included personal introduction videos, complete with backgrounds and interviews with the Four Seasons Private Residences Denver team members who would be caring for the resident once a home was chosen.

The advertising campaign was a record breaker. Click-through rates on the web ads came in at over 600% of the average web campaign. The website itself performed incredibly well with almost unprecedented amounts of time spent on site. "Hang-time" was over twenty minutes per visit, ten times that of the usual two-minute industry average.

And then came the qualified customers. The gamble paid off. Wealthy Finder buyers got the message and came calling. Their purchase intention already set by the campaign, they bought because of the product and the life that it offered – not the price. Four Seasons Private Residences Denver sold exactly as Chris Norton had planned – with one glaring diversion from that plan. It sold out in eight months, a year and a half ahead of schedule.

Let's return to Earth from the lofty heights of the 30th floor of a Four Seasons and talk about "real" real estate. The example shown here is relevant because the concept of product before price holds across a spectrum. Like any other example, real estate products cannot be easily transformed from Keeper to Finder product with just a website and a faintly life-affirming short film. If the home for sale is a vinyl-sided split level on a busy street, well, good luck getting any kind of an above-market premium. If, however, that home has, for example, a big old climbing tree for shade in the back yard, and a kitchen that opens out on to a deck in that yard, with maybe a fire pit that can double as a pizza oven, you might be on to something. Maybe it has an open plan and fiber-optic high speed Internet and a great yoga/ workout space. Then, you might just have a home that someone can fall in love with without getting hung up on price. There are so many variables that go into what people want in a real estate purchase. The trick with Finders is to travel in a direction where product does indeed come before price and build from there. When selling your home, think about how it reflects Finder values. Go back and read up on them in Chapter 6. If it does, you can stick to a price; the right buyers will find you.

36

NOT LOCATION NOT LOCATION NOT LOCATION

The New Grocery Getters

There is a question that exists in the retail business that is about as old as the knock-knock joke. Question: What are the three rules of retail? Answer: Location, location, location. So, if these really are the three rules, then here's another question – it's a longer one. Question: How does a business that is hidden in the very back of an industrial park, that is itself hidden about three blocks behind a suburban auto mall and located about thirty minutes from an urban center, become a place that has been pretty much lined up six days a week on a constant basis for the past ten years? Here is a hint: Not location, not location, not location.

Shades of Hansel and Gretel come to mind when thinking about Thomas Haas and his childhood. Thomas is a fourth generation pastry chef and chocolatier who literally grew up in his family's pastry shop in the heart of Germany's Black Forest. Yes, that is the same Black Forest that the cake is named after. As this particular candy-related tale goes, Thomas had quite naturally been expected to one day take over the family business.

Instead, he chose to walk down another path, one that took him up through the snakes and ladders of the European culinary scene leading to Switzerland and then France and then, with another story twist, to Vancouver as pastry chef for that city's Four Seasons Hotel. Soon, his talents attracted attention in a larger market and he found himself living in New York and working practically around the clock as pastry chef for famed French chef and restaurateur, Daniel Boulud. The New York culinary life was engrossing and all encompassing but Thomas wanted a little more, namely a better place to raise a family in a location that better fit his passion for hiking and cycling. So, he came back to Vancouver. When he got back to the rainforest city, he piled up his savings and bought into a small space in an industrial park. It was there that he would start his little chocolate factory. He put a retail counter out front as something of an afterthought. Since 2004, there has seldom been a time when there wasn't a lineup at Thomas Haas Chocolates and Patisserie. It is a lineup that now extends beyond that one obscure location to a second spot across town. Thomas' chocolates can be ordered online and you may find them, if you're lucky, placed carefully on your pillow at a few select Four Seasons Hotels around North America. The actual line, the one that leads in from the industrial park and through the front door to the busy counter, will include more than a few orders for double baked croissants or cappuccinos but it will always be more deeply motivated by those chocolates. Yes, the chocolates. There are the standards, the Earl Grey chocolate ganache or the caramel and fleur de sel.

There are the seasonal explorations such as a stout and malt crunchy praline made with Guinness. No matter what flavor of chocolate, customers are happy to jockey their cars for position in the tiny storefront's six tight parking spaces, or hike a few blocks down from the nearest street parking spot to pay a minimum of $2 each for what might be the best chocolate one could ever roll one's eyes in pleasure over. For our purposes, these chocolates, as delicious as they may be, represent something else and finally a different answer to those three rules of retail: Product, product, product.

Thomas Haas Chocolates has never needed to advertise. The product was so good that it was first discovered and then enthusiastically shared among the Finders who got there first. With his resumé and family history there is certainly much to be said for Mr. Haas' pedigree. That in itself is a great story but it would have amounted to nothing had his product not been the new definition of what a great chocolate could be in a rich port city that holds strong culinary roots and a collective palate that punches well above its weight.

No advertising, no direct mail, no in-mall sampling, no celebrity endorsements, and no discount coupons. Instead, Finders fell in love with those chocolates and then, Thomas, the passionate and personable master. Once indoctrinated, those same Finders came back with their friends. Those who didn't get it, those who didn't see the difference between a box of eighteen chocolates for $36 and a $3 bag of Dove minis, didn't come back. And that's a good thing, because those who did get it needed the parking spots.

Apart from the fact that both sell something we eat, a chocolate shop is a far cry from a grocery store. But Thomas Haas serves to illustrate what Finder food shopping is all about. A favored grocery store in a Finder's world is not a store that acts as a container to be filled with brands and commodities. It is instead something that begins with a set of definitive products and has a store built around them.

Finders and Groceries – Pretty on the Inside

Fiscalini Bandage Wrapped Cheddar. The 'bandage' bit might seem a bit gross but that little quibble is well worth overlooking when you consider that this straw-colored wonder has been voted the best farmhouse cheese in America for three years running. There's also handmade mozzarella, made fresh daily in the same location as the Fiscalini is sold. Then there are the 698 other cheeses that make up the total of 700 cheeses of the cheese department at the Houston, Texas Central Market.

There are nine Central Market stores spread around Texas. Each one has the same slogan printed on a sign outside. It is a line that gets repeated around the stores and on the website. It reads, "Really Into Food." This little chain, part of the larger San Antonio-based H.E.B. network, is an excellent example of the Finder grocery store. The fact that this slogan is absolutely telling the truth forms a big part of the reason why.

Central Market holds true to "Really Into Food" and

that makes it a Finders' food store. This truth-in-slogan is a refreshing departure from the normally fatuous role of that billboard and radio jingle dwelling piece of tag line fluff. In a world of hyped over-promise and apologetic under-delivery, it is easy to consider almost any advertising slogan to be just a bit of turd polish. In the case of Central Market, the slogan is different quite simply because it is demonstrably true. Central Market can honestly claim to be really into food not because they say they are but because they show that they are. Each store has its own in-house chef. The little chain goes out of its way to feature very hard to find foods and will take chances on the idea that a new food might not become an instant hit with customers. It is quite willing to take that chance, trusting in the idea that their own exploration of interesting and unusual foods will be shared, and ultimately bought, by a customer who holds similar interests and values.

With a full in-house kitchen, what you see at a Central Market is what they cook. The staff are trained to know a lot more about food than what you would expect from the usual aisle and checkout folks who might make eye contact with you at a Kroger or Safeway. To back up that product knowledge, every store conducts a series of cooking classes and wine classes. Also, there's live music on the weekends. Central Market is a pioneer in what is becoming a little more commonplace in today's grocery shop. The retailer was among the first to go with a fresh-over-grocery concept. In this model, packaged goods and their resident brands play a much smaller part in the layout of the stores. You can buy all of those items (or something approximating their equal) at Walmart anyway. Instead, there are fewer packaged goods aisles and more fresh bins and service counters.

Those increased bins offer the customer far more choice in fresh fruits and vegetables and allow for a wider selection of locally grown products and organic produce. This careful emphasis on fresh also extends to the counter service. Counter service, where goods are displayed behind glass and served by a staffer, is how a good food store like Central Market can replace pre-packaged, refrigerated, self-serve displays. This way, the purchase of meat, seafood, deli, cheese, and bakery items take place on a more personal level. By putting these fresh products at service counters, the customer gets much more of an opportunity to confer with staffers over everything including nutritional information, what's fresh, personal preferences, and even cooking tips. In doing so, real human relationships, not brand relationships, are born between store and customer.

For Central Market, "Really Into Food" is a simple and truthful statement of values that is constantly being manifested in the experience that a customer gets out of shopping there. Finders do not buy into advertising that tells them what to think, or brands that make claims on their labels ahead of the products contained within. Instead, they respond according to an alignment between themselves and what the seller is doing. Central Market does this. Then Central Market adds on to that

Finder-attractive quality by providing the Finder with deep dive information around what it sells. It gives its customers be-there-first opportunities with new and interesting products and puts them in highly sensory environments with that on-board kitchen and that out-sized fresh department. Finally, with all of those fresh service counters, Central Market builds the same sort of personal relationship that we saw all those chapters ago when Jessica went shopping at the Italian grocer. In a case of Finder meeting Finder, the staff at Central Market are people who "get" the customers who come to their counters, aisles, and checkouts.

Lost in Whole Foods

Central Market is most certainly not the only Finder foodie. There are of course the independents and the specialties and even much larger chains. Greensboro, North Carolina based chain The Fresh Market stands at 160 locations and growing. Then there is the store that has to be part of any Finder food shopping conversation, Whole Foods. To kick off, it is useful to note that according to businessinsider.com, shares in that natural foods powerhouse had fallen by 33% between November 2013 and September 2014. Where they go from there remains to be seen.

Whole Foods Market is many things and, yes, it is a good place to find Finders. There is no doubt that one can most certainly give a high score to the chain that has become synonymous with the concept of the high-end natural food store. Whole Foods Market is so dominant in its category that its name is a near synonym for the phrase "big expensive natural food store." In that way, Whole Foods is the Xerox or the Kleenex of its category. But therein, as the British might say, is the rub.

With an incredible selection of top-of-the-line natural foods, excellent seafood and meats sections, and a broad stock of interesting baked goods and specialty items, Whole Foods makes a strong case for itself as a great bunch of products with a good container built around them. Finder food heaven? Maybe. Before arriving at that conclusion, let's look at the product and price relationship. With the nickname "whole paycheck" and a customer who demonstrates a willingness to spend accordingly, Whole Foods might be the very definition of product before price. There's the problem. It is a strange kind of turnaround that is more than hinted at by the nickname. By being "whole paycheck," Whole Foods actually becomes about price all over again. Whole Foods Market sits at a solid point atop the grocery store pricing pyramid (real or perceived doesn't matter, perception always wins). This changes Whole Foods as a brand in a way that it is not seen so much as a definitive product but as a luxury brand. This is a kind of perception that planned or otherwise leaves an indelible mark on any brand. Be it the Stella Artois beer – one that was once quite successfully advertised as "reassuringly expensive" – or that perennial luxury brand Rolex, anything that speaks of its high cost is destined to become a status symbol. Whole Foods never went out and advertised itself that way; in fact by not advertising and thereby abdicating control of its own story, the chain actually created a vacuum where a segment of vocal and price-noisy customers could independently create and proliferate that rhinestone encrusted moniker. Advertised or not, the result was the same. Now, a Whole Foods Market grocery bag with its attendant association with high prices has become something more than a reusable earth-friendly sack; it has become a handy, all-purpose status symbol.

It is absolutely true that the products sold within a Whole Foods appeal to Finders in search of the best products in an information-rich and highly sensory environment, an environment that utilizes some excellent design cues. Yet once out the front doors and out in the world, the brand carries all of the, "Look what I can afford!" bragging rights that are sweet victory to the High Status Keeper. Does Alan, he of the wife with the temporarily non-diamond bracelet, love Whole Foods? You bet your grass-fed, free-range, organic ass he does. Its high prices are the only thing that could get him talking about grocery shopping.

Then there is the ubiquity of that same brand and the plain big bad wolf-ness of it. Most can recall a time before Whole Foods came to town. That was a time of funky natural food stores and organic butchers hidden in some out-of-the-way cheap retail space. In those days better food might have been hard to find, but getting it was a bit of an adventure. Some of these stores began to grow and flourish. They were the locally owned heroes of better food and a healthier planet. Traveling from that not-so-long-ago time to as-you-read-this today, you can observe that almost all of those stores are gone. They have, for the most part, been bought-out, driven out of business, or rendered obsolete by that giant natural food store. Or rather, that big giant natural food store brand.

That's enough picking on Whole Foods Market for the time being. There is much to be said for many of the "right-on!" values espoused by it. Whole Foods is ranked a consistent winner among America's best places to work. It has an employee healthcare program that, depending on how you vote, is either the model of how public/private healthcare could be run or the boogeyman that threatens a perfectly functioning status quo. Whole Foods gives back to local charities. It is a fact that Whole Foods has had more to do with the growth and viability of organic and pesticide-free farming practices in this country than any other single organization. Finally, Whole Foods has great food. Again, there is much to be said for its relationship with Finders and a certain alignment with their values. And, again, there is a problem.

This is where we return to Tina and those eggs of hers. Remember her? If Tina had been pushing her cart around a Whole Foods on a Sunday afternoon, she might have had even less to think about as she picked up that carton of "real-est" eggs. As she continued shopping, she would have filled her cart with all kinds of natural and real-authentic foods. The trouble is, the thrill would be gone. By being such a big brand, Whole Foods cannot help but turn itself into something removed from the chocolate with the shop built around it or that bandage-covered cheese with the grocery store built around it. Instead, Whole Foods becomes a brand that defines the outside of a store with a bunch of food inside that is simply assumed to be of a quality that Finders would love. By doing that, there is nothing new in it. Nothing new to discover. Nothing left to be…Found.

H-E-B Foods, the owners and operators of Central Market, enjoy a certain advantage that cannot be overlooked. They only operate in their home state of Texas. By being regional, the grocer remains relatable to its customer. This is something that Whole Foods, or for that matter, Kroger can never imitate. No matter how local those brands attempt to act, they remain national.

Roger Dooley is a contributor to *Forbes Magazine*. In a 2014 article titled, "The Smartest Supermarket You Never Heard Of," he observes and applauds a number of strategies employed by H-E-B to *delight* customers. Among these strategies are what he calls "freshness cues." Freshness cues include tricks of the trade that can be seen in the form of seemingly poorly organized and overflowing produce bins, or (and this is a common one at Whole Foods) fish that is aggressively displayed on sloped tables of crushed ice, displayed as such regardless of the fact that said fish has already been liberated from its head or even previously frozen. Then there is the handwritten chalkboard, a double-duty freshness indicator that hits the customer with the immediacy of an offer and a freshness cue at the same time. Yes, Finders do seek real authenticity and one could easily give these little tricks a shrug of dismissal except for one little fact: they work.

Dooley takes his report a step further with an amazing piece of data from market research firm Market Force. This is where the word "delight" actually gets its own metric.

Market Force talked to shoppers all over America and created a "delight index" by plotting consumer ratings of various supermarket chains against two metrics. One was "Satisfaction" and the other "Very Likely to Recommend." When a grocery store would score highly on each of these measures, that brand would find itself in the top right hand quadrant of the index – a good place to be. When it scored low on those two measures, it wound up in the bottom left – not a good place to be.

The winners? H-E-B and Whole Foods Market both found themselves up in that top right quadrant. Publix and even Target occupy the nearby territory. One brand reaches way beyond all of them and defines the very top right corner of the delight matrix by a margin so great that it looks like they cheated. Before we get to them, let us at least mention the grocery brand that defined the very (very) bottom left of this matrix. The store that scored the very lowest in the "Satisfaction" and "Very Likely to Recommend" matrices is Walmart. It would seem that shopping in an environment that is all about the lowest price comes with its own non-monetary price. The Delight Metric is even more telling and acutely Keeper indicative when combined with Walmart's market share. That share, in 2013, represented a whopping 25% of the total U.S. grocery market (Kroger came in at a very convincing second place). This means that during 25% of all grocery shopping trips that took place that year, customers were willing to get pretty miserable in order to get the deal.

When looking at the measures of satisfaction and willingness to recommend, it is worth reminding oneself that those metrics do not define Finders or Keepers. The state of being delighted means different things to each set. In this way, Finder or Keeper would respond to those questions in different ways with different sets of parameters that would inform their answers.

In any case, according to Market Force, the winner of the Delight Metric, by a huge distance is Trader Joe's.

A state of the commonplace is working its way into the natural and organic retail foods space. As the industry matures, more and more food retailers stock organic products and inevitably, price competition ensues. Meanwhile, organic and/ or ethically-sourced packaged goods brands are losing their unique selling proposition to newly arrived and equally organic parity products. This kind of growth is good for farming, for the environment and for the consumer but for a brand, it throws differentiation out the window. Trader Joe's doesn't fight this kind of parity. It makes the most of it by offering what are primarily house-brand versions of natural, organic and ethical brands at low everyday prices. That isn't to say that the stores contain nothing but house-brands; Trader Joes offers plenty of artisanal and locally-sourced goods – most of which can be found in the fresh sections that surround the grocery aisles. In this way Trader Joe's offers itself as a cheaper place to shop for organic, natural and ethically sourced products but manages to do so without becoming all about the discount. Look at it this way, if Trader Joes were all about price, Two Buck Chuck would be $1.97 Chuck.

Finders will pay more for something different and something that lives at the peak of real authenticity: the definitive product. This holds true for groceries as much as it does for a Subaru. It still doesn't render the whole grocery category irrelevant; it simply means that because of its widened availability, Tina and her tribe have adopted natural food shopping as a matter of course. Now her grocery-related pleasure centers are a little harder to stimulate. To get the real lift, she will go to that one-off ethnic store, farmers' market, specialty butcher, or even go so far as to buy eggs at the farm gate. Given the time and the right conditions, she will do all of the above. This is because Whole Foods has managed to take a broad swath of Finder coveted foods and turn them into everyday products under one roof thereby creating an interesting new level of commoditization. With this, the everyday Finder grocery shop has become a little less special and a little more about price. That is where Trader Joe's comes in and wins.

Go All the Way or Go Away

Grocery shopping is a big deal – a big deal as in $945 billion spent in the U.S. in 2011. Naturally, an industry this big comes equipped with plenty of competition. There is no end to the strategies, maneuverings, and grenade-throwing contests that take place in grocery's endless race for competitive edge and differentiation. It all takes place within a trade that is, more often than not, apples versus apples. With that particular table set, it comes as little surprise that this is also an industry that can often be seen as trying to straddle the worlds between Finder and Keeper. In the grocery trade, like in any other, the territory in between is a killing ground. Most of these attempted straddle maneuvers are created and then driven by divergent forces. One is the force of quality and the other, that beloved grocery store claim, the lowest price.

Just for old time's sake, let us go back to Tina and Lloyd's supermarket and push a cart around a few aisles. As you travel down the canned soup aisle, you might spot a big pre-printed and brightly colored tag reading "ONE DAY ONLY SPECIAL." If you hung around for a while, you would see that other customers will often pick up a few cans of soup from behind that tag without much thought. Sales tags remain powerful triggers to all of us as we travel through the less romantic part of a shopping trip in a state that nears catatonic. There it is, a strong price driver that works.

Then we will round a corner to the produce section to see a variety of artfully hand-drawn chalk signs and a line of straw baskets filled with fresh apples and peaches. A second signal fires off that supports a bunch of fresh and wholesome choices. Great. Apples and peaches are welcomed aboard the cart.

Both of these moves are common to the grocery chain but the second one presents most grocers with a problem. Those signs are expensive to create and constantly recreate. Forgive the obvious here but expensive equals cost, and cost equals either lower profits or higher prices. Now, if that grocery store, like so many in its category, feels a need to claim the lowest price, it will have to give up on the artsy-fartsy bits. Some try to have it both ways. This is where we encounter the pee-in-your-own-pants-to-feel-warm compromises that so many retailers, grocery or not, will impose on themselves. Here is how it will unfold. A design firm is hired to create a new concept grocery store to compete in the newly burgeoning Fresh and Organic segment. A fresh-feeling signage and identity package is created for the stores. In sort of a "farmhouse chic" style, it calls for handwritten sales tags, plenty of chalkboards, hand painted aisle and directional signage, and vintage neon signage over the meat, fish, and bakery counters. By looking at the sketches and 3D renderings, the client can see that a land of fresh at premium prices has been created.

Then comes the collision between price and design. It comes from this kind of statement, "We want to offer a fresh shopping environment while beating our competitor's prices." Budgets that reflect such cost cutting are then created accordingly. Instead of vintage neon for those service counters, cheaper backlit signs with a neon style typeface are created. Handwritten signs are replaced by a faux handwritten typeface. Chalkboards are replaced with stock illustrations and another faux chalk typeface on pre-printed, chalkboard-masquerading Coroplast board. Those hand painted aisle signs are recreated in vinyl. Thousands of dollars are saved in fixed costs and more in ongoing costs with the elimination of in-store artists. The outcome in the minds of the company bosses is a store that looks "just fresh enough" to allow for a slightly premium price. Management applauds the added profit potential as big-packaged-good brands line up to pay rebates for positions on end-aisle displays. A large LaserJet printer is installed in-store to print out daily specials on that same stock illustration artwork in that same handwritten style typeface. A big sales event, complete with opening specials, launches the store and we're in business.

A year later, the store is a riot of laser printed specials taped to every available surface. Stacks of Diet Coke and Cheetos sit under the faux-handwritten, faux-farmhouse-style aisle signs. The store is losing money. Of course it is. The store that claims to be authentic and cheap at the same time can only really claim one thing. The middle.

Finders can spot a fake a mile off, and Keepers are just as good at spotting a bad deal. This new brand has created a place that gives its hoped for high-value customer all the signals of artifice. Instead of a farmhouse, it feels like a tacky plastic farmhouse with sensory cues that make the food seem about as fresh and genuine as a can of spray cheese. One visit from a Finder and even if the fakery has not been consciously registered it has been absorbed and rejected. Design shows you care; execution and materials prove it.

Those Keepers will have a different but similarly negative reaction. They will encounter a bunch of irrelevant decorations that aren't even real enough to be worth paying more for and run back to a place that doesn't let a store full of frills get in the way of a cart full of deals.

Trader Joe's has a strong perception around low prices but it chooses its battles. You can't buy Trader Joe's Cereal anywhere else. In this way they get to set the rules in their own pricing game, and they define prices against Finders and not Keepers. Sure Trader Joe's might be seen to have lower prices but not to a died-in-the-wool Keeper who would reject an eighteen ounce canister of Trader Joe's Organic Oven Toasted Oats at $2.69 for a $3.98, forty-two ounce silo of what she would see as exactly the same thing in its trusty Quaker Oats brand form at Walmart. For Trader Joe's, and for that matter Whole Foods Market and Texas' Central Market and Canada's Fresh Street Market, aiming at the correct customer comes with a willingness to deliver on the product and then build the right environment around it.

Grocery, fashion, housewares, automotive; no matter what industry, never try to have it both ways. Go all the way or you will go away.

37

I'M NOT HERE:
FINDERS AND THE INTANGIBLES

"I'm sorry sir we can not take that hold off of your ATM deposits before the waiting period has elapsed."

"But I've been with your bank for fifteen years and you have never done this before."

"It's a new policy. We have to confirm the funds."

"You have! That check was from my wife! The funds have already been taken from her account!"

"I'm sorry Mr. (mispronounced name) but we must hold your ATM deposit for five to seven working days."

"But I have checks clearing on that account. They'll bounce."

"I'm sorry…" (Here it comes…) "It's company policy."

"(Silence)"

"Sir?"

Company Policy. There might not be another phrase in the English language that draws a more distinct line between customer and uncaring institution than that one. Get overcharged on your cell phone? Company policy. Get denied an insurance claim? Company policy. Get berated by a power-mad airline company gate supervisor? Company policy.

Is there such a thing as a Finder aligned service-based company? A free-range cell phone company? An artisanal insurance company? An organic bank? Before we leave the farmer's market analogies aside, it is well worth asking ourselves if there is a part of our spending, the service part, that could be a little more authentic and a little less programmed. A little less "company policy."

How did it come to this? Before we begin to rail against the big corporations or the uncaring shareholder, let us instead get out the remote control, grab a refreshing beverage and maybe a few snacks, turn on the TV, and settle onto the sofa. Our assignment? Find a car insurance commercial that isn't about the lowest price. Here's hoping you packed lots of snacks. Next, try and find a travel website that didn't guarantee the same thing. While we're at it, look for a cell phone company that doesn't claim to have the lowest price or the best value or the best package and/or the freest device. It hasn't always been this way and, armed with the internet, we consumers have set ourselves as the drivers of a world of low prices, lower prices, and nothing but lowest prices. As a result, all of these services have simply run out of anything else to sell except for the lowest price. With the lowest price, like any other product, comes the lowest quality. Lowest quality in service means lowest-cost call centers, long waiting lines, and the real enemy of service, use of policies over training, or worse, use of corporate policy over common sense, discretion, or real empowerment.

You may have noticed that banks were left out of this examination. This might seem interesting because, generally speaking, banks make all kinds of profits and are not under constant siege from competition. Banks seem like just the sort of places where at least a Finder sub-brand might flourish. That does not seem to be the case. Instead, banks seem to live in a state of self-imposed commoditization. Maybe there is just one conclusion at work here, they are banks.

Then there is Zappos, the online shoe retailer with insanely good service. Zappos' very existence seems to speak in the opposite direction of Finder buying. Think of our R.M. Williams Boot shod Finder, Frank, back at the Costco. Remember Frank? We can just imagine Frank at some very interesting men's shoe store, trying those new boots out on the recycled wood flooring in some barely retail, post-industrial part of town. Getting the same sort of boots online just wouldn't have the same sense of place or depth of experience attached to it. Would it? No, probably not. Instead Frank would just get insanely great service with this simple mission statement, "To provide the best customer service possible."

Today, Zappos can get your order shipped within eight minutes of that final transactional mouse click. Shipping is always free. That of course is a policy that actually benefits the customer. Staffers have no limits on the time that they can spend with a customer and are totally (run a mental hi-liter through this next word) empowered to make any decision that supports the happiness of a customer. For those of you who have followed that company's story, Zappos is the poster child for service. Much has already been written on this quite revolutionary company that sells somewhere in the neighborhood of $2 billion worth of shoes every year. Any student of great service culture owes it to herself to study the brand long and hard. But for our purposes, the Zappos story isn't the point. The point is the fact that so few service based companies have had the intelligence to simply copy the Zappos cultural model and move it into their own industry. After all, somebody somewhere can always beat Zappos on price. They just can't beat them on service. So here comes the question: Why isn't there a Zappos of insurance, cell phone, cable, or online travel services or, for that matter, banking?

Empowered Service and the Finder Effect

Jake and Daryl have big man names, which is fitting because Jake, the smaller of the two brothers is 6'4" and weighs in at a solid 260 lb. Daryl weighs 20 pounds more but that makes sense because he's an honest three inches taller than his older brother. It's been about thirty-five years since these two shared a room much less a bed but as the door closes behind them and the lights go on the very subject of a shared bed reveals itself. They had booked a single room with two king-sized beds. They got a single room with just one king-sized bed. Both take a moment to size up the bed and let the reality of the situation sink in. Jake is the first to break this contemplation. He picks up the room phone, punches the zero, and gets the front desk.

In ten minutes the two have been upgraded to a small suite; complimentary appetizers and cold beers are on the way. And, of course, the suite has two king-sized beds spaced nicely apart thank you very much. It had all happened so quickly, so easily, and so well that the two are experiencing a sort of post-service vertigo. Even the beginning of the process seemed odd. For example, when Jake made the call he only talked to one person and he wasn't put on hold – not for a moment. He didn't hear a conversation take place between desk clerks on the other end of the line. The problem was simply solved. This brief inconvenience had been erased and reversed with uncomplicated precision.

What the brothers encountered was the magic of the empowered employee at a Ritz Carlton Hotel. Every single employee at every Ritz has the same level of baseline empowerment. That empowerment means that any employee, from chambermaid to desk clerk to manager, is able to spend up to $2,000 of the company's money, no questions asked, to keep any single guest happy. It is a "company policy" that works brilliantly in the opposite direction of the conventional expectation of those two dreaded words.

In a Finder's world what this kind of empowerment means, be it a waiter's ability to take a disappointing dinner item off the check or a store clerk's independent ease at taking back a pair of pants, is a shared sense of personalization between buyer and seller. Empowerment means a clean and non-bureaucratic, non-authoritarian interface between the two sides of the transaction. If you were to consider the peer-to-peer relationship that is created by a shared love of food between staff and customers at Central Market, there is a parallel that exists in the category of services that is created by employee empowerment. In this case, a peer-to-peer relationship is created that is akin to a shared rejection of an institutional style chain of authority. The customer and the seller experience freedom together.

Then there is another, deeper level of engagement that occurs between Finder and empowered employee. This sort of employee has been invested with a similar level of authority as those further up the corporate or company structure. This means that the customer is actually dealing with a level of proxy for the originator of a given service. Going back to the example of our reluctant bedfellow brothers, their interaction and ultimate delighted satisfaction that came from one call to a desk clerk meant that they were actually connected to the top of the Ritz Carlton Company. In a sort of parallel universe to a Finder taking a trip to the farm gate, employee empowerment allowed Daryl and Jake to go "straight to the source" in getting a better hotel experience.

This brings us to the crux of the Finder and service relationship. No matter what they do, Finders will always be Finders. Finders are always in search of a real connection to whatever it is they are purchasing. They seek tailored solutions that fit their exact and individual needs. They reject the authoritarian one-size-fits-all prescription – the sort of company policies that serve the seller ahead of the customer. Finders are all about self-determination, so the idea of being forced to deal with any company that blocks the freedom to operate in this context is pure kryptonite. When you look closely at a huge service-based company like Zappos, or a strong and scalable service culture such as what can be found at Finder-attractive retailers and restaurants – those who cross-pollinate their great products with incredible service – you will see a set of characteristics that are consistently delivered. As a customer, you might not see Finder aligned service in a concrete or even a conscious form. That is the magic. They're there – you just can't see them. You feel them.

38

◆

FINDER CARE

Creating a Finder Service Culture is hard. Hard and worth it. To make it all a little easier, let's cover it in steps.

1. **Empowered Staff:** Empowerment works on three levels. First, it creates a conduit that brings the customer to the top of the service food chain, to the source. Secondly, it removes the company versus customer relationship that places a repellent level of authority in front of the Finder customer. Thirdly, it attracts a Finder employee. Finders and Evolving Finders are self-directed careerists who embrace flexibility. An environment of empowerment attracts them to the job where they are far more able to understand, react to, and anticipate the needs of their Finder customer counterparts.

2. **Real, Meaningful Missions (RMM):** "To provide the best customer service possible." "Every Customer Leaves Happy." "Creating Experiences That Amaze People." "Radical Ease of Use." These are real, meaningful phrases, the first, Zappos, the second, that of a successful premium casual restaurant chain, the next, a tourist

attraction company, the fourth, well, if you don't know this one, try Googling it. (It's the first Apple mission statement.) In each case, it is easy for members of the organization's team to know what they came to work to do every day and then deliver on it. The RMM creates the very simplest of decision trees where the empowered employee can act independently while referring to a one-commandment scripture as an operating guideline. RMMs are the opposite of the generic, buzzword-burdened, and unmemorable corporate mission statements. As one extremely successful and Finder-attractive restaurateur who built his empire on service puts it, "Carry strong values and a thin rule book."

3. **Singular Accountability:** Peter was the publisher and owner of a thriving community newspaper but he had a problem. Every single member of his management team and many of his staff would see him as the fixer, the answer man, and the solution to all of their problems. Seldom was there a moment in his working life when there wasn't a line up at his office door – until the day he put up a sign outside of this well-used office door. It read: "Never for a moment think that you work for anyone but yourself." The line went away. Accountability in service means that every single member of the company is accountable to deliver the company's RMM and, of course, its product. Singular accountability creates a reluctance to let go of a customer

and pass that person to another staff member. For a Finder, this is experienced as both a lack of bureaucracy and a sense of personal service coming from the one person who will now champion her needs. Singular accountability means that every member of the team can be that "one person." But more than all of the other points, this one does not work without deep knowledge and training which brings us to...

4. **Train to Expert:** Customer: "I'm torn between the lamb or the chicken. What do you suggest? Waiter: "I'm a vegetarian." Finders want to know more. A company can only deliver on that deep level of information when every member knows everything there is to know. About everything. Using that little restaurant scenario, it is of fundamental importance that at any company, be it an online clothier or the booking line for a cat-skiing guiding company, every single person knows not just "what's on the menu" but the ingredients, the source, provenance, seasonality, up-to-the-minute situation, and best accompaniments to those "menu" items. In the Finder company, new hires aren't just job hires; they are career hires. They are carefully selected and creatively recruited talents. Employees are hired to fit and to be a critical part of a long-term team. They are invested in, trained to win, and truly valued. They are nurtured to be the definitive example of great service. And if they're not, they're fired.

5. **Hire the Finders:** Entrepreneurial Evolving Finders have their best customers in Finders. This extends to the Finder company. Finders have their best service relationships with those who get them. Given the wide gulf in values between Finders and Keepers, there is little to be gained by trying to force a square-peg-round-hole interface between company and customer by staffing it with Keepers. Any organization that qualifies to be a Finder-aligned company gets there by having a product that is both definitive of its category and has values that align with its Finder customer. The same of course must be said of the values of those who work there, particularly, but not by any means exclusively, those who deliver service.

And Finally, Be a Finder Company

All of the above points will simply ring hollow if the company is, in its DNA, a Keeper company. There is simply no way to invest in service or to be relevant to a Finder if the company just isn't a Finder company.

39

BUILT FOR FINDERS

We have travelled through the heights of Subaru, Anthropologie, and Lululemon. We have waved at Apple and said hello to Four Seasons Private Residences. We have gone shopping with a Finder and followed a Finder career. We've seen some very impressive statistics around the spending power of Finders. So now it is time to open our organic artisanal lemonade stand or fine-tune our company to become a Finder-beloved business juggernaut. Or not. Let's find out.

THE FINDER COMPANY SELF -TEST

Question 1 and Rule #1

This is the Quidditch Question. If you have read your Harry Potter, you will know that J. K. Rowling's wizard game has one pretty deep flaw, it doesn't really matter how many goals either team scores in a game (each goal scored counts for fifteen points). The real win comes when the Golden Snitch is caught, giving the Snitch-catching team an instant 150 points and, effectively, the victory. If you have not read Harry Potter or seen any of the movies, you may now shake your head in confusion from the safety of whatever rock you hid under between 1998 and 2012. In any case, to run a Finder company, you have to be a Finder. That's the 150-point, you-caught-the-Golden-Snitch answer. Everything else is important, but without that, there is no victory to celebrate over flagons of butterbeer.

Be a Finder or be a Keeper. You can't have it both ways. It is easier to get a sex change than it is to change from Finder to Keeper or Keeper to Finder. At the risk of being over simplistic, a person who would get a sex change is doing so because what they are on the inside doesn't match what they are on the outside. What a Keeper is on the outside is what a Keeper is on the inside. What a Finder is on the outside is what a Finder is on the inside. Go back to the Finder and Keeper spotter guides back in Chapters 5 and 8. Look for yourself, look for key members of your management and/or ownership team in those identifiers. Don't waste your time deluding yourself. Be brutally honest. Here comes the all-important question:

Question 1

Are you a Finder or a Keeper?

Finder ☐   Keeper ☐

Question 2

2a) Your mission statement: Is it something that sounds like this? "Creating excellence and customer satisfaction while profitably maintaining the best/biggest etc. etc. etc. blah blah blah."

Yes ☐   No ☐

2b) Or something like, "Creating experiences that people are amazed by."

Yes ☐   No ☐

2c) Do you know your mission statement and what it means without having to look it up?

Yes ☐   No ☐

Question 3

Is your product a definitive product? One that others try to recreate but cannot in terms of clear, sustainable superiority, in terms of technology, design, service culture, provenance, materials, craftsmanship, and/or other meaningful dimension?

Yes ☐   No ☐

Question 4

Are you highly vulnerable to price competition?

Yes ☐   No ☐

Question 5

Are your company's culture and values aligned with that of your customer? For example, do you make or do something that you would like made or done for yourself?

Yes ☐   No ☐

Question 6

Does everyone – or at least the vast majority of your staff, management, and team members – feel that same value and cultural alignment with customers?

Yes ☐   No ☐

Question 7

Does anybody hate you? *

Yes ☐   No ☐

* If that last one threw you, here's a hint:

By definition, when you make something no one hates, no one loves it. ~ Tibor Kalman, 1949 – 1999. Noted American graphic designer and former Editor in Chief, *Colors Magazine.*

Question 8

Do you really need to advertise to stay in business or will your business grow on a different set of merits?

Yes ☐   No ☐

Question 9

Do your competitors want to be you? (As opposed to you wanting to be them.)

Yes ☐   No ☐

Question 10

Are your customers happy to pay more for your product, or don't really care about your prices? (within reason of course).

Yes ☐   No ☐

Question 11

Do the members of your team at every level of the organization feel that they are on a common mission, that they are part of something?

Yes ☐   No ☐

THE SCORE

Question 1

Finder = 150 pts

Keeper = 0 pts

Question 2

2a) Yes: 0 pts
   No: 15 pts

2b) Yes: 15 pts
   No: 0 pts

2c) Yes: 15 pts
   No: 0 pts

Question 3

Yes: 20 pts
No: 0 pts

Question 4

Yes: 5 pts
No: 15 pts

Question 5

Yes: 15 pts
No: 0 pts

Question 6

Yes: 15 pts
No: 0 pts

Question 7

Yes: 15 pts
No: 0 pts

Question 8

Yes: 0 pts
No: 15 pts

Question 9

Yes: 15 pts
No: 5 pts

Question 10

Yes: 15 pts
No: 0 pts

Question 11

Yes: 15 pts
No: 0 pts

If you scored...

300 – 335   You are a Finder Company. Congratulations. Where do we invest?

275 – 295   You are probably a Finder Company. Go back to the beginning and read this book again.

200 – 270   You could be on your way to being a Finder company. There is much work to be done.

Under 200   Conflicts abound between Finders and Keepers, values and product, or any combination of the sets. It is unlikely that you are getting a lot of sleep.

Under 150   You are a Keeper company or you are in the dreaded world that sits between Finder and Keeper. Go all-the-way Keeper or make a career change.

CONCLUSION

There is no time machine.

If you live in a town that still has a newspaper, you might want to look at the center advertising section that usually comes out on the weekend. There is an excellent chance that you will find it filled with starburst and headline-bejeweled car ads. If this is true, it is equally likely that you will find, in different ads, two or three versions of exactly the same car bearing exactly the same claim of the lowest price. If you're lucky, you will find a comparison chart somewhere that lists all of the features that this car comes with. It will be a chart that extolls the brand's superiority over other brands by sheer number of features. What you are really seeing here is not a sure-fire advertising strategy built to bring in customers who are undoubtedly as excited about these deals as the headlines are; instead you are seeing an attempt at time travel. These ads are simply an effort to enter a time machine where the car dealer can travel back to a bygone day when a brand, a set of features, and a special offer meant a lineup of ready customers on Saturday morning.

Turn on the TV and see a McDonald's spot where untold numbers of delicious calories can be had for a small price that

always ends in 99. Turn it off and wonder why sales at the golden
arches continue to fall.

Life used to be so simple. Advertising told us what a brand
was; a price told us what it was worth; a sale price told us to buy
it now; and a set of features made that brand's product better
than the other brand. It all worked for a few decades. It worked
until everyone started to do exactly the same thing.

It worked until those who had money to spend, and enjoyed
spending it, didn't really care anymore. Those people moved on.
They stopped believing the hype, they started looking for the
products that fit them on their own terms, and they stopped
settling for a compromise wrapped up in a deal.

Some businesses really understood those customers and
became successful. Some businesses were run by the same sorts
of people and had the good fortune of attracting a like-minded
and ready-spending customer. Some businesses decided that
they had to make a choice between lowest price and highest
quality and made the right choice.

Some perished.

Some just kept looking for a time machine.

FINDERS & KEEPERS AND MORE

This book is a beginning. The value of the Finder cannot be fully explored over every industry in real time within its pages. As a customer – and even as a donor, voter, or citizen – the Finder can have a profound impact on everything from ice cream to neighborhood planning to mobile phones. With this in mind, Finders & Keepers exists in blog and video formats and is regularly updated at thefindersandkeepers.com.

You can find the author and his partners at:
rob@thefindersandkeepers.com
richard@thefindersandkeepers.com

ACKNOWLEDGMENTS

Christopher Norton

I, along with my team, would like to extend a humble and heartfelt thank you to Christopher Norton, without whom this book would not exist. Chris introduced us to the concept of the NEO and the Traditional, hired us to work with its teachings, and went out and put its theories into practice. His own book, *One Hundred Thirteen Million Markets of One*, has been a constant companion during this writing. He'd probably hate this nickname but we think of Christopher Norton as the Socrates of Santa Barbara. Chris, may the sun shine on you and may your wildest dreams be achieved beyond your wildest dreams.

Richard Bergin

Almost every word of this book, and certainly every indecipherable pre-edit sentence, has been read to Richard out loud, usually uninvited, and in an endless series of thoughtless interruptions. His patient advice, enthusiastic support, and deeply informed insights have helped propel what began as a 1,800-word white paper into what you see now.

James Filbry

Someone has to keep the ship moving. Spring Advertising Partner and Associate Creative Director, James Filbry, has performed the awkward tasks of both steering the ship and shoveling the coal while this member of the crew has been off surfing in the wake. Thanks for your fine captaincy and fearless work ethic, James. We couldn't have dodged those icebergs without you.

Clients Big and Small

To work in the advertising business is to work in every business that advertises. And some that don't. So thanks to that now out-of-business chain of home electronics stores, thanks to that insurance company, that grocery chain, that fashion brand, and that organic baby food company. Thanks to the juice company, the convenience store chain, and the car brands from Korea, Japan, and America. Thanks to the restaurant chain that never advertised and the beer company that never really needed to.

We learned almost everything from you.

ABOUT THE AUTHOR

Rob's career in advertising began at age six where he earned his allowance by cleaning the production department at his parent's community newspaper. He is creative director, and a founding partner at Spring, an advertising and design shop based in Vancouver, Canada. His creative work has been recognized by Communication Arts, London International Awards, the One Show, the Clios, and the Webbies. Rob is an occasional copywriting instructor, a frequent guest speaker on strategy and creativity in communication, and the lead singer of the mid-life crisis pop-punk band, the Dadolescents.

"100 Best Companies to Work For 2013- Zappos.com - Fortune."
Fortune Magazine. Time Inc., N.d. Web. 20 Jan. 2015.

"About Us." Airbnb. N.p., N.d. Web. 20 Jan. 2015.

"About Us." Anthropologie. Urban Outfitter Inc., N.d. Web.
16 Jan. 2015.

Anthropologie - LinkedIn. LinkedIn Corporation. Web. 16 Jan. 2015.

Arden, Paul. *Whatever You Think, Think the Opposite.* New York:
Portfolio, 2006. Print.

"Audi Brand Sales Figures." Good Car Bad Car. N.p., N.d. Web.
14 Jan. 2015.

"Auto Sales - Market Data." *The Wall Street Journal.* Dow Jones &
Company Inc., 5 Jan. 2015. Web. 17 Jan. 2015.

Bartlett, John. *Familiar Quotations: A Collection of Passages, Phrases
and Proverbs Traced to Their Sources in Ancient and Modern
Literature.* 15th ed. Boston: Little, Brown, 1968. Print.

Baertlein, Lisa. "UPDATE 1-Whole Foods Sales Accelerate, Shares
Rise." Reuters. Thomson Reuters, 11 Feb. 2015. Web. 23 June
2015.

Berger, Jonah. *Contagious.* London: Simon & Schuster, 2013. Print.

"Cadillac Brand Sales Figures." Good Car Bad Car. N.p., N.d. Web.
14 Jan. 2015.

Cain, Timothy. "2009 U.S. Vehicle Sales Rankings." Good Car Bad
Car. N.p., 27 Mar. 2013. Web. 16 Jan. 2015.

Cavendish, Lucy. "The Gastronauts: London's New Breed of Restaurant-goer." *The Telegraph.* Telegraph Media Group, 9 Oct. 2012. Web. 15 Jan. 2015.

Central Market. Network Solutions LLC. Web. 19 Jan. 2015.

"Chevrolet Malibu Sales Figures." Good Car Bad Car. N.p., N.d. Web. 14 Jan. 2015.

"Chevrolet Volt Sales Figures." Good Car Bad Car. N.p., N.d. Web. 14 Jan. 2015.

"Circuit City Lets Go 34,000 Employees as Doors Close for Good." Salem News. N.p. 8 Mar. 2009. Web. 16 Jan. 2015.

Collins, James C. *Good to Great: Why Some Companies Make the Leap…And Others Don't.* New York: HarperBusiness, 2001. Print.

Dodge, Shyam. "January Jones Splashes out on Lavish $1.7 million Home in Los Angeles with Its Very Own Backyard Zip-line and Swimming Pool." *Daily Mail UK.* Associated Newspapers, 30 May 2014. Web. 16 Jan. 2015.

Dooley, Roger. "The Smartest Supermarket You Never Heard Of." *Forbes.* Forbes Magazine, 28 Jan. 2014. Web. 15 Jan. 2015.

Euromonitor. Grocery Retailers in the US. London: Euromonitor International, 2014. Ebook.

"Financial Information." Lululemon. Lululemon Athletica Canada Inc., 23 Jan. 2015. Web. 23 Jan. 2015.

"Frequently Asked Questions." Toyota Mobility. Toyota Motor Sales, N.d. Web. 17 Jan. 2015.

"George Bernard Shaw." *The Guardian.* Guardian News and Media Ltd., 28 July 2008. Web. 24 Jan. 2015.

Gladwell, Malcom. *Outliers: The Story of Success.* New York: Little, Brown & Company, 2008. Print.

"Global B2C Ecommerce Sales to Hit $1.5 Trillion This Year Driven by Growth in Emerging Markets." EMarketer. EMarketer, 3 Feb. 2014. Web. 16 Jan. 2015.

Gretler, Corinne. "Freitag Brothers Tick Swiss Fashionistas' Fancy With Biking Bags." Bloomberg. Bloomberg, 24 July 2012. Web. 20 Jan. 2015.

Griswold, Alison. "Why Chipotle Customers Don't Care About Rising Burrito Costs." Slate. The Slate Group LLC, 19 May 2014. Web. 15 Jan. 2015.

Gundzik, Jay. Personal Interview. 15 Aug. 2014.

"Honda Brand Sales Figures." Good Car Bad Car. N.p., N.d. Web. 14 Jan. 2015.

Honeywill, Ross, and Verity Byth. *NEO Power: How the New Economic Order Is Changing the Way We Live, Work and Play.* Carlton North: Scribe Publications, 2006. Print.

"Howard Schultz Profile." *Forbes.* Forbes Magazine, 19 Jan. 2015. Web. 19 Jan. 2015.

Jaws. Dir. Steven Spielberg. Perf. Roy Scheider. Universal Pictures, 1975. DVD.

Jones, Adam. "Chipotle Mexican Grill's Double-Digit Revenue Growth." Market Realist. Contact Privacy Inc., 18 Dec. 2014. Web. 19 Jan. 2015.

Kakuk, Amy, Beth Theriault, and Jessica Bourgoin. "American Airlines AMR Inc." N.p., 2004 PowerPoint Presentation. Web. 16 Jan. 2015.

Kalman, Tibor. Interview with Brad Wieners. "Wired 4.12: Color Him a Provocateur." *Wired Magazine*. Condé Nast Publications Inc., 1 Dec. 1996. Web. 23 Jan. 2015.

Keyes, Allison. "Circuit City Stores Set To Close For Good." NPR. NPR, 8 Mar. 2009. Web. 16 Jan. 2015.

Lamotta, Lisa. "Wal-Mart Scoffs At Recession." *Forbes*. Forbes Magazine, 5 Mar. 2009. Web. 16 Jan. 2015.

"Largest Private Companies: #114 Linen N Things." *Forbes*. Forbes Magazine, 9 Nov. 2006. Web. 16 Jan. 2015.

Lee, Adrian. "Lululemon Boardroom Fight Is a Corporate Culture War." *Macleans*. Rogers Publishing Ltd., 1 July. 2014. Web. 14 Jan. 2015.

Lesova, Polya. "Target June Same-store Sales down 6.2%." Market Watch. Dow Jones & Company Inc., 9 July 2009. Web. 16 Jan. 2015.

Lindstrom, Martin. *Buy-ology: Truth and Lies About Why We Buy*. New York: Broadway Books, 2008. Print.

"Loxcel Starbucks Store Map." Loxcel. N.p., 27 Nov. 2014. Web.

16 Jan. 2015.

"LULU Annual Income Statement." Market Watch. Dow Jones & Company Inc., Web. 23 Jan. 2015.

"Lululemon: Women's Bodies Are The Problem." *The Huffington Post.* AOL Canada Corp., 6 Nov. 2013. Web. 13 Jan. 2015.

Lutz, Ashley. "Whole Foods Is Making 6 Changes To Improve Business." *Business Insider.* Business Insider Inc. 22 Sept. 2014. Web. 15 Jan. 2015.

Marati, Jessica. "Investigating The Ethics Of Anthropologie's Made In Kind Project."EcoSalon. Organic Authority LLC, 25 Apr. 2012. Web. 16 Jan. 2015.

McGrath, Maggie. "Red Lobster And Olive Garden Drag Darden Lower." *Forbes.* Forbes Magazine, 20 Sept. 2013. Web. 15 Jan. 2015.

Menashe, Jeff. "State of the Craft Beer Industry 2013" Demeter Group Investment Bank. Network Solutions LLC, N.d. January 8, 2015.

Mint. "Eat, Drink, and be Thrifty: Track Your Spending with Mint Personal Finance Software." Online video clip. YouTube, 6 April. 2011. Web. 16 Jan. 2015.

Moretti, Enrico. *The New Geography of Jobs.* Boston: Houghton Mifflin Harcourt, 2012. Print.

Nelson, Jr. Keith. "Vinyl Sales Surpass 9 Million for the First Time in 20 Years as Streaming Breaks Record." Digital Trends. Digital

Trends, 2 Jan. 2015. Web. 19 Jan. 2015.

Neumeier, Marty. *The Brand Gap: How to Bridge the Distance between Business Strategy and Design* - A Whiteboard Overview. Rev. ed. Berkeley: New Riders, 2006. Print.

Neumeier, Marty. *Zag: The Number One Strategy of High-performance Brands* - A Whiteboard Overview. Berkeley: AIGA, 2007. Print.

"New Automotive News Data Center." Automotive News. Network Solutions LLC, N.d. Web. 17 Jan. 2015.

"New Study Finds More Than 20 Million Yogis in U.S." *Yoga Journal.* N.p., 5 Dec. 2012. Web. 24 Jan. 2015.

"Nissan Brand Sales Figures." Good Car Bad Car. N.p., N.d. Web. 14 Jan. 2015.

Norton, Christopher, and Ross Honeywill. *One Hundred Thirteen Million Markets of One: How the New Economic Order Can Remake the American Economy.* Minneapolis: Fingerprint Strategies, 2012. Print.

Patton, Leslie. "McDonald's Profit Drops 30% as U.S. Sales Slump." Bloomberg. Bloomberg, 21 Oct. 2014. Web. 19 Jan. 2015.

Perez, Sarah. "ITunes App Store Now Has 1.2 Million Apps, Has Seen 75 Billion Downloads To Date."TechCrunch. TechCrunch, 2 June 2014. Web. 16 Jan. 2015.

Poon, Aries, and Karen Talley. "Yoga-Pants Supplier Says Lululemon Stretches Truth."WSJ. Dow Jones & Company Inc., 19 Mar. 2013. Web. 13 Jan. 2015.

"Previous Years - Best Global Brands - Interbrand." Best Global
     Brands. Interbrand Group, N.d. Web. 14 Jan. 2015.

Reiss, Robert. "How Ritz-Carlton Stays At The Top." *Forbes*. Forbes
     Magazine, 30 Oct. 2009. Web. 20 Jan. 2015.

Schultz, Howard, and Dori Jones Yang. *Pour Your Heart Into It:
     How Starbucks Built a Company One Cup at a Time.* New York:
     Hyperion, 1997. Print.

Schultz, Howard, and Joanne Gordon. *Onward: How Starbucks
     Fought for Its Life Without Losing Its Soul.* New York: Rodale,
     2011. Print.

Smith, Ethan. "Music Downloads Plummet in U.S., but Sales of
     Vinyl Records and Streaming Surge." WSJ. Dow Jones &
     Company Inc., 1 Jan. 2015. Web. 19 Jan. 2015.

"Story." FREITAG. Ascio Technologies Inc., N.d. Web. 20 Jan.
     2015.

"Subaru Brand Sales Figures." Good Car Bad Car. N.p., N.d. Web.
     14 Jan. 2015.

Taylor, Alex. "Are Subarus the Best Cars Money Can Buy?" *Fortune
     Magazine.* Time Inc., 19 Nov. 2012. Web. January 8, 2015.

"Tesla Model S Sales Figures." Good Car Bad Car. N.p., N.d. Web.
     14 Jan. 2015.

"The Bombay Company, Inc. Company Profile, Information,
     Business Description, History, Background Information on The
     Bombay Company, Inc." Reference for Business. Advameg Inc.,

N.d. Web. 16 Jan. 2015.

"The Bombay Company Launches at Fred Meyer." *Alaska Business Monthly*. Alaska Business Monthly Magazine, 28 Apr. 2011. Web. 17 Jan. 2015.

"The House That Lululemon Built." Luxury Homes. Vertical Properties Inc., 12 Aug. 2014. Web. 16 Jan. 2015.

"Toyota Brand Sales Figures." Good Car Bad Car. N.p., N.d. Web. 14 Jan. 2015.

"Trader Joe's Is Consumers Favorite Grocery Chain." Market Force. Market Force Information, 24 July 2013. Web. 15 Jan. 2015.

Trudell, Craig. "GM U.S. Dealer Profit Surges to 9 in 10 Validating Cuts." Bloomberg. Bloomberg, 30 Sept. 2013. Web. 17 Jan. 2015.

Tuttle, Brad. "America's Most Popular Supermarket Is Also Its Least Loved." Time. Time Inc., 2 Apr. 2015. Web. 22 June 2015.

Ueland, Brenda. *If You Want to Write: A Book about Art, Independence and Spirit*. New York: G.P Putnam's Sons, 1938. Print.

"Unemployment in October 2007: The Economics Daily." U.S. Bureau of Labor Statistics. U.S. Bureau of Labor Statistics, 6 Nov. 2007. Web. 16 Jan. 2015.

"Unemployment in October 2009: The Economics Daily." U.S. Bureau of Labor Statistics. U.S. Bureau of Labor Statistics, 10 Nov. 2009. Web. 16 Jan. 2015.

"Urban Outfitters – Trefis." Trefis. 9, Insight Guru Inc., 19 Aug. 2014. Web. January 9, 2015.

Weber, Harrison. "Apple Averages more Sales per Square Foot than Any Other U.S. Retailer (study)." VentureBeat. Venture Beat, 16 May 2014. Web. 17 Jan. 2015.

"What Is Kickstarter?" Kickstarter. Kickstarter, N.d. Web. 20 Jan. 2015.

Young, Angelo. "Elon Musk In Detroit: Tesla CEO Visits Auto Show After GM Unveils Future Model 3 Challenger." *International Business Times*. IBT Media Inc., 13 Jan. 2015. Web. 20 Jan. 2015.

CPSIA information can be obtained at www.ICGtesting.com
Printed in the USA
LVOW06s0722220915

455191LV00001B/36/P